Troy History Reader

Volume One

Don Rittner

Dedicated to
Christopher R. Rittner

ISBN: 978-0-937666-72-2

©2022 Don Rittner
All Rights Reserved

No part of this publication may be reproduced, stored in a retrieval system, or transmitted in any form or by any means, electronic, mechanical, photocopying, recording, or otherwise without prior permission

Published by
New Netherland Press
Schenectady NY

Table of Contents

Introduction, 1

Norman Rockwell And Troy Made Beautiful Art Together!, 3

Boy Scouts, Detachable Collars, and a Troy Connection?, 23

Cannon Place is a Le Grand Building!, 31

Will the real Uncle Sam stand up!, 39

You better run for you life, 53

You must be nuts to write a dictionary, 61

Troy Building once an early printer and school, 65

From Lindy's Alley to City Station, 69

For whom the bell tolls?, 75

Helen Finally Comes to Troy, 81

What To Do with Troy's City Hall?, 91

X didn't always mark the spot, 99

Yes, Virginia, there really WAS a Santa Claus, 109

Missed Opportunities, 113

Cohoes Falls An Ancient Wonder of the New World, 117

Uncle Sam's Uncle Tom, 129

Abolitionist Stoned in 1836 by Trojans, 135

Yes Virginia there was Rock and Roll in the Capital District, 139

Monument Square in 1905 before the Hendrick Hudson Hotel replaced the Mansion House seen here.

Introduction

Growing up in Troy in the 1960s was a magical time. It was before urban renewal and the demolition of hundreds of historic buildings that ripped the guts out of the business center. Thousands of people shopped and lined the streets on the weekends. There were so many people in downtown you had to walk down the street because the sidewalks were full. Downtown was full of department stores, restaurants, shoe stores, jewelry stores, clothing stores, theaters, you name it and you could buy it in Troy. As a kid, I use to throw a magnet on buildings that later I learned were cast iron storefronts made by Troy iron foundries. It all came to a crashing end during the 1970s and beyond.

For twenty years (1999 to 2007 — 2009 to 2021), I penned a local history-centered column that appeared in the *Troy Record* and the *Albany Times Union* newspapers in the Capital District region of New York State. Over these two decades, I tried to educate the public on the unique history that makes up the capital region since it was here that American history began when the Dutch built a small fur trading fort on an island in 1614, now part of the City of Albany, the present Capital of the State.

In these two decades, local politics has allowed the continual destruction of much of our valuable archaeological, historic, and ecological sites. While I wish I could say it is uncommon it has been the standard operating procedure of many communities in th Capital District. Native Americans called it home for thousands of years until they were displaced by events of the 18th century. They understood their relationship with their environment. Not so with the later European mentality that proclaims the Earth and its resources are for the taking, no matter the cost.

In this ancient area, you should expect to find a great deal of history to uncover and promote. Many writers before me have done so and many will in the future. Why is history important? Obviously knowing it can save one from making the same mistakes. It only takes burning your hand on the stove once to realize that it is precious information and will make you think twice about doing it again. Every human creates their individual history and collectively provides information that can help move us forward. Knowing history, especially your local history, provides a sense of place, a familiarity, or security of mind when you go about your daily life. The more I learn about my neighborhood the more secure I feel living in it.

I am republishing a selection of my stories that I feel are useful or interesting especially for newcomers to Troy, and even old timers. In Volume One you will find articles about Norman Rockwell's relationship with Troy, how Troy promoted anti-slavery, the real story of Uncle Sam, and the connection between the early founding of the Boy Scouts and Troy's collar industry, to name a few of the eighteen stories in this edition.

I have always said that Troy is a magical city. The more you learn about the people that have made Troy one of the wealthiest and productive cities in America during its first two hundred years, the more impressed you become. The city was a magnet for inventors, scientists, writers, artists, and most other categories you can imagine. You will find a Trojan in almost every major American historical event from the American Revolution to the Industrial Revolution and beyond.

Like most Northeastern cities, Troy fell on hard times as the 60s flight took place and people went to the suburbs and downtowns and businesses disappeared. Urban Renewal destroyed hundreds of great buildings and replaced them with grass or parking lots. However, in the last couple of decades a newer generation has found Troy to be a great place to relocate, work, and raise a family. Most of the vacant buildings in downtown have been revitalized and now contain small independent businesses, like former times. The younger crowd has positive feelings about the walkability of the city, what is left of its historic infrastructure, and they embrace the history. Even Hollywood is finding Troy to be a great backdrop for feature film and television productions.

Troy has a great future ahead of it as long as politics doesn't put up barriers as they have in the past.

History changes by the day. One can only hope that what you do today will be looked back on as a contribution to the progress of human society so that its final chapter can be one that made it worth its existence.

Troy's early mantra was *Ilium Fuit, Troja Est* (Ilium Was, Troy Is). A more fitting tag today would be *Troja semper erit* (Troy will always be).

Don Rittner
July 2022

Norman Rockwell And Troy Made Beautiful Art Together!

First published on August 8, 2011, at 11:56 PM

I have always considered Norman Rockwell one of the best illustrators of all time. He captured America and its culture during the post-war of the 1940s to the 70s. His covers for *Saturday Evening Post* and later *Look Magazine* for 40 years and his work for the Boy Scouts made him a household name. Living in nearby Stockbridge Massachusetts, Rockwell would often drive to nearby "big" cities like Troy, NY, and Bennington, Vermont for inspiration and photograph landmarks to use in his paintings.

There have been a number of his works that feature a Troy landmark or streetscape in one way or another either directly or by influence. Let's take a look at some.

The Street Will Never Be The Same – 1952. Produced for Ford Motor Company.

In 1952 Ford Motor Company commissioned Rockwell to do a painting celebrating their 50th anniversary. It would later appear in a 1953 calendar. Rockwell chose a street scene in Troy and after looking at a few locations chose a three-building set on Fourth Street with 296 Fourth being the central focus. In the painting, he placed a Model A and horses and wagons on the street and workers on the two flanking buildings.

Today there is a historic marker honoring the three buildings that remain. I guess the street has remained the same after all.

The Street Was Never The Same. Source: Internet.

Three buildings used by Rockwell on 4th Street.
Photo by Don Rittner

Rockwell's photo showing the Troy buildings as they were, 294, 296, and 298 4th Streets. Source: Norman Rockwell Museum Digital Collection. Copyright 2011 NRELC.. Licensed by Norman Rockwell Licensing, Niles, IL

1953 Ford magazine ad. Source: Internet

Ford 50th anniversary Calendar. Source: Internet

Another similar almost identical building he photographed. Source: Norman Rockwell Museum Digital Collection. Copyright 2011 NRELC. Licensed by Norman Rockwell Licensing, Niles, IL

Walking to Church
Produced for the April 4, 1953 issue of the Saturday Evening Post.

Rockwell's Walking to Church. Source, Internet.

The Silver Slipper at 2279 5th was a three story, not two as depicted in the painting. Source: Norman Rockwell Museum Digital Collection. Copyright 2011 NRELC. Licensed by Norman Rockwell Licensing, Niles, IL

The Silver Slipper today. Housing instead of dining. Photo by Don Rittner.

Most sources I have read attribute this painting as a composite of Troy, Cambridge, NY, and Bennington, VT. There are obvious elements in this painting that are Troy. Rockwell took several photos in Troy for possible use in the painting. Photos of 5th Avenue between Fulton and Grand which contain brownstones and the First United Presbyterian Church at 1915 5th Avenue, for example. The steeple of this church can be seen in the middle of the painting behind the Silver Slipper. Supposedly the church steeple on the left is from Bennington but Rockwell did take photos of St Pauls on Third Street. I see no evidence of it in the painting, however. The two-story Siver Slipper Grill in the painting was located near Hoosick at 2279 5th Avenue but had a name change to the Silver Dollar Grill (there was also a Silver Star Restaurant at 18 King St). It also was a three-story building, not two. The building on the right is from another location as Rockwell's photo of the buildings shows a different style (I'm looking for it). His insertion of a barber shop on the building on the right could have been inspired by the barber shop at 271 4th St. The location was then known as Dolan's (Mom and Pop) and Pat's Barber Shop. These Rockwell photos of 271 4th were included in his catalog of shots belonging to the Walking to Church painting.

St Paul's and Barker Park. Source: Norman Rockwell Museum Digital Collection. Copyright 2011 NRELC. Licensed by Norman Rockwell Licensing, Niles, IL

Fifth Ave and Grand Street. First United Presbyterian Church. Source: Norman Rockwell Museum Digital Collection. Copyright 2011 NRELC. Licensed by Norman Rockwell Licensing, Niles, IL

Unknown Troy location for Walking to Church. Source: Norman Rockwell Museum Digital Collection. Copyright 2011 NRELC. Licensed by Norman Rockwell Licensing, Niles, IL

Dolan's and Pat's Barber Shop (271 4th). Source: Norman Rockwell Museum Digital Collection. Copyright 2011 NRELC. Licensed by Norman Rockwell Licensing, Niles, IL

Dolan's and Pat's Barber Shop (271 4th), north side. Source: Norman Rockwell Museum Digital Collection. Copyright 2011 NRELC. Licensed by Norman Rockwell Licensing, Niles, IL

271 4th Street today. Photo by Don Rittner.

The Homecoming
Produced for the May 26, 1945 issue of the Saturday Evening Post.

One of my favorite Rockwell paintings is of the GI coming home in 1945 after the war. This painting was based on the backyard of 1715 7th Avenue just a few doors north of the present county health department building (the house site is now a parking lot). There is no 7th Avenue today as it was wiped clean by urban renewal in the 1960s-70s. Rockwell added the GI and people in the painting. Look at the stark contrast with his real photo below.

When Rockwell was sketching the rear of 1715 7th Avenue, 18-year-old June Larkin had just come home from work at the Watervliet Arsenal and saw a man sketching her building. She asked if she could watch him and he agreed and asked her to stand on the side of the house. She had no idea it was Rockwell until the next year when she saw herself on the cover of the Saturday Evening Post.

The Homecoming with Troy's June Larkin standing on the left side in the dress.

Returning Soldier Troy. Rockwell's photo of rear of 1715 7th Ave. Source: Source: Norman Rockwell Museum Digital Collection. Copyright 2011 NRELC. Original negative was reversed on web site. Licensed by Norman Rockwell Licensing, Niles, IL

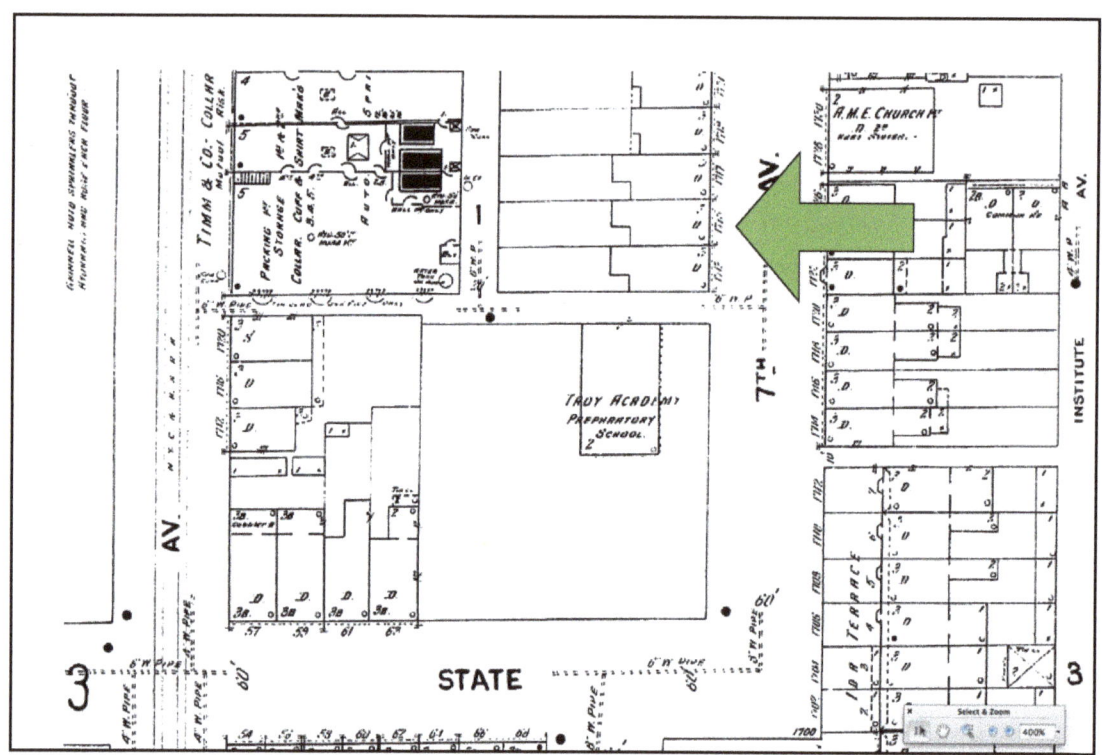

Sanborn Map of 1715 7th Ave. Source: Sanborn Map 1953.

1715 7th Ave is now a parking space. Photo by Don Rittner.

Saying Grace. Produced for the November 24, 1951 issue of the Saturday Evening Post.

Saying Grace. Norman Rockwell. Source: Internet

Rockwell's photo of the Burden Iron Complex used in Saying Grace. Source: Norman Rockwell Museum Digital Collection. Copyright 2011 NRELC. Licensed by Norman Rockwell Licensing, Niles, IL

Saying Grace was another composite of Rockwell's. The interior was shot in his home while the industrial background was the Burden Iron Complex in South Troy. He took photos of the complex and inserted the gas house, industrial building, and a NY Central Railroad Engine and cars as the window background.

Unknown Photos

In the Rockwell collection are photos that do not have locations or are attributed to a particular painting although I am sure they are of Troy. I have identified a couple of them and the unidentified ones I post them here for your help. If you can identify the location, let me know and I will post it.

B-Lann Equipment
2295 5th Ave.

B-Lann at 2295 5th Ave. Source: Norman Rockwell Museum Digital Collection. Copyright 2011 NRELC. Licensed by Norman Rockwell Licensing, Niles, IL

B-Lann which specializes in fire suppression and personal protective equipment is still in business at their location at 2295 5th Avenue in Troy.

K-C Grill
2266 5th Ave

K-C Grill at 2266 Fifth Ave. Source: Norman Rockwell Museum Digital Collection. Copyright 2011 NRELC. Licensed by Norman Rockwell Licensing, Niles, IL

K-C Restaurant is now the site of a community gardens. Photo by Don Rittner.

K-C was a popular bar and restaurant on 5th Avenue not far from King Street.

Unknown Location #1

Do you know where this is? Source: Norman Rockwell Museum Digital Collection. Copyright 2011 NRELC. Licensed by Norman Rockwell Licensing, Niles, IL

This photo shows a slightly sloping road and so could be a side street going up towards Mt. Ida (Prospect Park) somewhere in South Troy. It appears that all three buildings may be wood sided or two brick-sided with the "vinyl" siding of the day (asbestos-backed sheeting).

Unknown Location #2 NOW IDENTIFIED AS 73 Hill Street

There were 157 bars and grills and restaurants in the city in 1953. Which one is this? One of my readers directed me to 73 Hill Street and sure enough, this is the building. It was Hartnett's Grill in 1949 and Roti's Restaurant in 1957.

Do you know where this is? Source: Norman Rockwell Museum Digital Collection. Copyright 2011 NRELC. Licensed by Norman Rockwell Licensing, Niles, IL

Now identified as 73 Hill Street. Here is the photo taken today.

Unknown Location #3 IDENTIFIED – 1645 5th Ave.

The two-story house with the dormers, is sandwiched in between two with boxes, but where is it?

Do you know where this is? Source: Norman Rockwell Museum Digital Collection. Copyright 2011 NRELC. Licensed by Norman Rockwell Licensing, Niles, IL

1645 5th Ave. When Rockwell took a picture of this building in the 1950s this part of 5th Ave was a neighborhood with several homes on both sides of the block. Now the few remaining buildings are boarded up or in disrepair. Photo by Don Rittner.

WE FOUND IT. One of my readers named Stephanie directed me to the location. This is 1645 5th Avenue between State and Congress. This section of buildings is now in a run-down condition and the one on the right 1647 has I believe a condemned sign on the window! What a difference fifty years makes! [Update. It has been renovated.]

Unknown Location #4

Does the sign say grocery or laundry? There seems to be a large grassy area behind this site, so perhaps off First Street?

Do you know where this is? Source: Norman Rockwell Museum Digital Collection. Copyright 2011 NRELC. Licensed by Norman Rockwell Licensing, Niles, IL

ALBANY

It also appears that Rockwell visited Albany as I found one negative that showed Albany from Erie Blvd, or Street (former Erie Canal) looking west. You can see the Capitol, Alfred Smith building, and Union Depot.

Albany through the eyes of Norman Rockwell. Source: Norman Rockwell Museum Digital Collection. Copyright 2011 NRELC. Licensed by Norman Rockwell Licensing, Niles, IL

Boy Scouts, Detachable Collars, And A Troy Connection?

First published on December 30, 2020, at 9:21 PM

Chances are everyone knows a Boy Scout or two. This youth-building movement began in London back in 1908. It was brought to America shortly after by W. D. Boyce, an American newspaperman, who after being aided by a London scout thought it would be a great program for kids in the US.

After returning to America in 1910 he joined up with Edward S. Stewart and Stanley D. Willis and incorporated the Boy Scouts of America on February 8 of that year. Boyce was encouraged to take it nationally by Edgar M. Robinson, a leader of the YMCA in New York City, and offered financial help. That year the Woodcraft Indians led by Ernest Thompson Seton, the Boy Scouts of the United States headed by Colonel Peter Bomus, and the National Scouts of America headed by Colonel William Verbeck were absorbed into the new Boy Scouts of America. The first office was opened in New York City on June 1, 1910, in the 128th street YMCA building. By the fall they had applications for leaders in 44 states and 150,000 requests from youths. The National Council was formed in the fall of 1910 with Colin H. Livingston as the national president and Robinson becoming the managing secretary. Seton became Chief Scout and wrote 'A Handbook of Woodcraft, Scouting, and Life-Craft,' the original Boy Scout Handbook.

You can download the original here:https://archive.org/details/boyscoutsofameri00seto

So who was the first official Boy Scout Leader? On September 19, 1910, only three months after the Scouts became official, Simeon F. Lester of Troy, New York, became the very first person to hold the Scouting leadership position of Scoutmaster that was approved by the BSA. He received his certification from the BSA headquarters in New York City. Lester was already working on a Scout program earlier. During three weeks in July 1910, he led a group of 63 boys at Camp Ilium, in Pownal, Vermont.

Camp Ilium was the starting point of the Boy Scout Movement for Troy, and Pownal is only 35 miles away from Troy. Camp Ilium began in 1908 on Barber's Pond at Pownal. The camp was used for eight years and then moved in 1918 to Camp On-Da-

Wa on a rented site on Crooked Lake in Rensselear County until 1921. That was replaced by Camp Van Schoonhoven on Burden Lake.

Lester eventually moved to Wellsville and headed the Allegany County YMCA and died at his home in Middlesex in 1937.

While at Troy Lester lived at 100 Seventh Avenue in Lansingburgh and worked for the YMCA on First Street in Troy.

The *Troy Semi-Weekly Times* on Tuesday, August 6, 1910, discussed the founding of the Troy Boy Scouts in an article about the opening of the Lake George Ernest Thompson-Beton Camp (In 1910 Ernest Thompson Seton became chairman of the founding committee of Boy Scouts of America). The camp was new and its purpose was to: *"advance the work of the Scouts of America in the Young Men's Christian Association."*

The article goes on to say:

The Movement in Troy
The Boy Scout Movement was started in the Troy Association [YMCA] at Camp Ilium and has met with great favor. The following members qualified as tenderfeet:

Arrow Collar Man. (1905-1931) was a fictional man that became an iconic image and male sex symbol for selling collars and cuffs and shirts from the Cluett Peabody, Company in Troy. He was used to sell more than four hundred different types of detachable collars. The icon was developed by Calkins and Holden, a NY Ad agency, along with Charles Connolly, Cluett's ad man and well known illustrator Joseph C. Leyendecker. The Arrow Man was in fact Leyendecker's real life companion Charles A. Beach who he met in 1903 and was hired by his older brother Frank Leyendecker also a magazine illustrator. Leyendecker was famous for his more than 300 covers of *The Saturday Evening Post* (like Norman Rockwell) between 1896 and 1950 but his famous 'Arrow Man' was known to receive his own fan mail and marriage proposals at the rate of a thousand a week. The Arrow Collar Man was one of the most successful advertising campaigns in US history. The popularity of the Arrow Man was the inspiration for George Kaufman and Marc Connelly's hit two act play Helen of Troy, NY, also starring Helen Ford, who was born in Troy. The play was performed in Troy for the first time in 2015 and directed by Don Rittner and Justyna Kostek.

Walter MacNey, Daniel C. Lester, Cornelius S Bullions, John A. McCullough, Alfred Haword Craig, William H. Demers, Willard H. Myers, Earl Hughes, Waldo V Dater, James G Schauwecker, Carl H Ruether, Walter Vause, Charles Harold Schauwecker, William D. Forster, Job F. Lyon, Chester H. Clifford, James L. Smith, H. Grant Stevens, Nelson P. Lund, George H. McCarthy, Walter S. Hogben, James Lloyd Handy, Floyd K. Inch, Raymond Griffin, Paul Neal, Ayers Holloway, Charters McQuide, Walter Nichols and Harold McChesney.

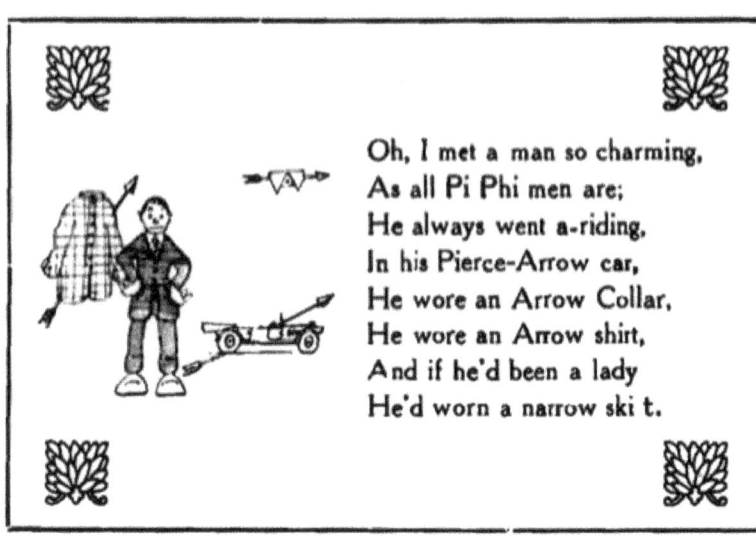

The Future Work Secretary S. F. Lester of the local association has been appointed Scout Master of Troy by John Alexander of New York, who is at the head of the movement. [Alexander was a YMCA administrator from Philadelphia – DR.] "The work will be vigorously pushed at the close of the vacation season. Those who have qualified as tenderfeet are making excellent progress toward the next step when they will become second-class scouts. Scout Master Lester is arranging a three-day outing from September 3-5. He is receiving many inquiries for information about the association rooms. Mr. Lester said today the purpose of the camp at Lake George was to make the fellows well acquainted with the movement and produce results after their return."

Scouting was not universally accepted in Troy or elsewhere and particularly with the Catholic Church. They did not like it since it was founded by the YMCA, a protestant based organization. In the *Albany Evening Journal* of September 25, 1911, it was reported that:

"The Rev Msg John H. Swift, pastor of St. Patrick's church announced from his pulpit yesterday that he did not want any of his parishioners to allow their children to belong to the Boy Scouts as he said, the Scouts were an auxiliary of the YMCA. When interviewed he is said to have stated that the warning was for his people only. The movement was a good thing for Protestant boys, he said, but he did not favor the organization seeking recruits among Catholic children."

That didn't catch on, fortunately.

But Troy's influence on the Boy Scouts does not end there. There is another Boy Scout First. The Boy Scout uniform so familiar across America was designed by Troy's Charles M. Connelly. He also helped design the scout badge and various other marks and insignia now familiar in the scouting world.

Connelly was the editor of the Chicago Trade journal, *The Haberdasher*. But Cluett, Peabody & Company, the giant collar maker of Troy, hired him to become their advertising manager. He lived at 25 Locust Avenue in Troy. The first thing Connelly did was to ask his artist friend Joseph Christian Leyendecker whom he had worked with in Chicago to work up an ad of a man in an Arrow collar. In 1907 the Arrow Collar Man, the ideal young American with the broad brow, frank eye, prow-like jaw, and cleft chin (not to mention Leydendecker's model was his gay boyfriend Charles Beach) for many years forward wore his clothes "with aplomb" and was the first American dream man and succeeded in making Arrow collars (over 400 types) the badge of the well-dressed man. Nine out of ten American men wore a Troy-made collar. Arrow collars and shirts were the sign of excellence.

For example, in *Drift,* the Butler University (Indianapolis, Indiana) yearbook of 1917, their Pi Beta Phi emblem had this saying (emphasis on arrow theirs):

He took her in a Pierce-Arrow Car;
He wore an Arrow collar;
He wore an Arrow shirt;

And if he had been a lady
He would have worn an Arrow skirt.

Troop 1 Boy Scouts from Troy Orphan Asylum was the first uniformed scout troop in the country. Designed by C. M. Connolly. Photo 1939, Vanderheyden.

C. M. Connolly's home at 25 Locust Avenue should have a historic marker on it. Photo by Don Rittner.

Simeon Lester, America's first official Scoutmaster, should have a historic marker at his 100 7th Ave. Burgh house. Photo by Don Rittner.

Another version of this is found in the 1921 college yearbook *Chinook*, from Washington State University:

The Arrow Collar and Arrow Collar man became part of the American lexicon during the 1920s through 40s. Lyrics from Irving Berlin's song "Puttin' on the Ritz" include the line *"High hats and Arrow collars…"* in the second verse, 1946 version. Watch Fred Astaire sing it here (27 seconds into it, but watch the whole video for fantastic tap dancing):

Try watching this video on www.youtube.com

Troop 1. Troy Orphan Asylum. Circa, 1920. Courtesy Vanderheyden.

Pool tables at the YMCA on First Street, c, 1920

YMCA on First Street, c, 1915

https://www.youtube.com/watch?v=GKPMk5_gStk

or Cole Porter referred to "Arrow Collars" in his song: "You're The Top" from the 1934 musical *Anything Goes* (you can hear it here sang by Porter himself in about 2:00):

https://www.youtube.com/watch?v=i6oGytt0Hiw

Lyrics sung by Julie (Hollie Bliss) in F. S. Fitzgerald's comic one-act play "Porcelain and Pink" from the 1922 short story collection Tales of the Jazz Age include the lines *"When the Arrow-collar man / Meets the D'jer-Kiss girl."* In Season 2, Episode 9 of the TV series 30 Rock, Jack Donaghy is described by Liz Lemon's father as *"looking like an Arrow Shirt Model"* after he's stunned by Jack's appearance.

There is even a modern *Arrow Collar Man* song by Sonic Kimono a 2011 psychedelic rock band from St Albans, UK.

You can listen to it on Sonic Kimono:
https://sonickimono.bandcamp.com/track/arrow-collar-man-3

Connelly also held a patent for a collar display device that he received in 1927. Connelly served on the Boy Scouts of America Committee on Permanent Organization and Field Supervision and was a member of the National Council and is listed in the first official handbook for boys. He was also on the Committee on Badges, Awards, and Equipment and helped design the Merit Badges and other items as well.

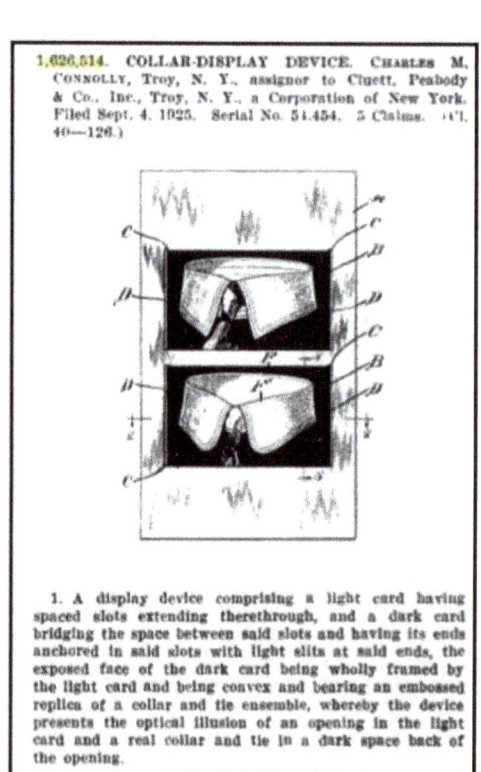

So not only was Connelly responsible for the look of the Boy Scouts, his advertising acumen made Cluett Peabody and Co. one of the largest and most successful collars and shirt companies in the world. The Arrow Collar Man was the most successful advertising campaign in the world and the Boy Scouts became one of the largest organizations for boys.

Cannon Place Is A Le Grand Building

First published on December 9, 2011, at 7:21 PM

The Capital District is the oldest continually settled region in the United States and contains hundreds of landmark architectural wonders. Cannon Place, located in Monument Square in downtown Troy, New York is one such landmark. It is the oldest structure in the square that once was known as Washington Square in the 19th century.

The lots that became the Cannon Building go back to the original founding of Troy. Lot 131, which comprised an area of 50 by 130 feet was leased on March 10, 1789, by Jacob D. Vanderheyden to Mathias Vanderburgh at a yearly ground rent of three pounds five shillings. It then went to Elias Lee, Nathan Betts, Nathan and Stephen Warren, Eliakim Warren, and finally on October 13, 1831, to Le Grand Cannon. Before the Cannon Building was opened on January 1, 1835, there stood one of the city's popular inns, a two-story wooden building from 1806-1814 known as the Bull's

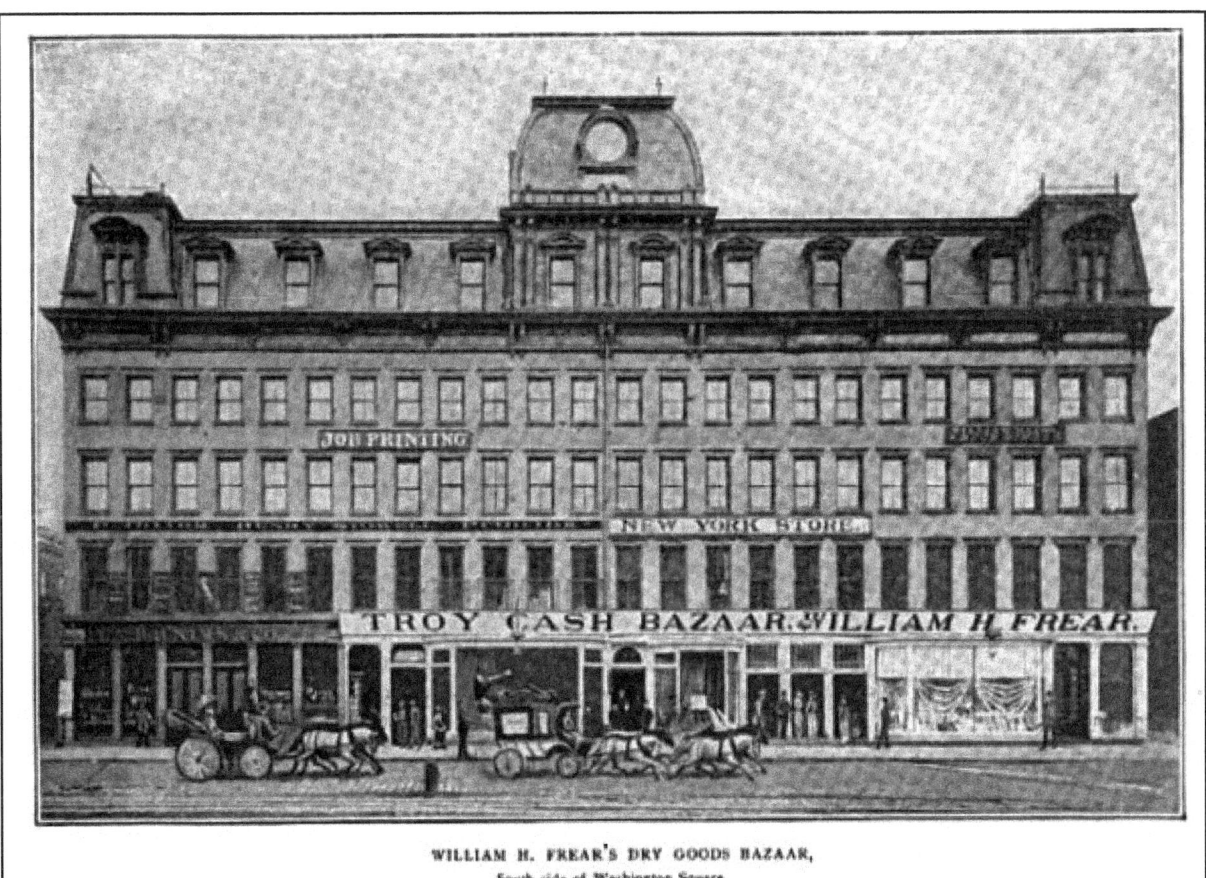

The Cannon Building around 1890. From Troy's One Hundred Years.

Head Tavern, kept by Elias LaSalle. There was a Bull's head sign hanging out front. Later it became a grocery store on the first floor by Daniel Oatman until Cannon purchased the property. The Cannon Building was built in 1834 and originally consisted of 8 stores 4 stories high with freestone fronts. It was designed by Alexander Jackson Davis in the Greek Revival style. Davis collaborated with Ithiel Town on the building's Greek Revival style producing a rare surviving large-scale commercial building in GR style.

Actress Charlotte Cushman performed once in the Cannon Building. Photo from the Net.

A fire in March 1854 blew out the firewall of Cannon Place and several buildings downtown were destroyed by the fire in which winds fanned the flames. A fire on March 13, 1869, nearly destroyed the building starting in the A. W. Scribner's job printing office. Moore & Nims, Clegg & Neber, Flagg & Frear, C.H. billings and Chas. Rising & Co. all took losses. On April 17th, Moore & Nims dissolved their partnership and reopened as H. B. Nims & Co with H.R. Nims, R. B. Moore, and H. T. Smith.

After the two fires, one in which all the records of the Troy Citizen's Corps were lost (Le Grand was a charter member), the mansard roof, usually associated with that era's Second Empire style was added in 1870.

1893 Nims Ad for globes.

For several years, the hall in the Cannon Building was rented to persons giving concerts and exhibitions. Before she became famous Charlotte Cushman entertained an audience there as a singer. She won rave reviews in Albany in 1839 doing Lady Macbeth. Her legendary lesbian affairs were well known in Europe where she spent much of her life.

Several well-known businesses

occupied the Cannon Building. The Troy Daily Times was first issued on Wednesday afternoon on June 25, 1851, and was published at number 5 Cannon Place from June 25, 1851, to January 7, 1853. At 9 Cannon Place, in 1842, W & H Merriam opened a bookstore. Nims & Knight took it over on February 1, 1886. Franklin Globes were produced throughout the second half of the 19th century in Troy by a succession of globe makers and sold by booksellers: Merriam & Moore, Merriam Moore & Co., Moore & Nims, H. B. Nims & Co., Nims & Knight, and back to H. B. Nims & Co. who sold them in the 1890s. They were available in the six, ten, twelve, sixteen, and thirty-inch diameters, with a variety of bases, generally in iron or wood and reflecting the prevailing Victorian decorative art style of the period. Ive's New York Store (clothing) was in number 3 & 4 Cannon Place in 1865.

Worthington & Phelps sold musical supplies at Number 2 Cannon Place in 1865. Fisk & Avery Printers were there until they moved west selling all their printing equipment in 1856. Hayner & Shaw attorneys had their offices there in 1870.

Le Grand Cannon came to Troy from Norwalk Connecticut and married Esther Bouton. Both individuals were of Huguenot Stock; she was descended from the Seneschals of the Fortresses of Dole in France, and he was from the founders of the New Rochelle Settlement in NY. His pew was at St Paul's church.

Cannon was the proprietor of the Conduit Company of Troy which supplied water to the city. They constructed a reservoir in 1833 in the Piscawen Kill. Le Grand was one of the principles and on April 18, 1829, the company was incorporated as the Troy Water Works Company. It sold its rights to the city on March 20, 1832. In 1833 construction of a dam and reservoir began

A popular item was the Globe sold by Nims. Photo from the Net.

Moore & Nims Ad, Troy Weekly Times, January 14, 1865.

and was completed in 1834, with 448,838 gallons capacity, distributed to the city by about four miles of pipes. Two more reservoirs were built. In 1843 and 1853 other reservoirs were constructed on the Piscawen kill west and east of Oakwood Avenue.

Cannon was president of the Rensselaer and Saratoga Railroad. The railroad was incorporated on April 14, 1832, and built a track from Troy to Ballston Spa, a distance of 24 miles. He was one of the first directors. The road was constructed in 1833 and on October 6, 1835, Tuesday, the first passenger train crossed the bridge between the city and Green Island and began regular operation leaving Troy every morning for Burrough (Mechanicville) in the Ballston and Saratoga railroad cars, precisely at 10 AM, and from there to Whitehall in coaches and the "splendid" new packet *Red Bird*. Cars would remain opposite the office of the company at 10 First Street and at the East end of the bridge every morning from sunrise to 9 o'clock to take freight from the Burrough to Ballston and Saratoga. From the bridge, the track extended down River Street to First Street and terminated in the yard on the South side of the two-story brick building then standing on the North part of the site of the Athenaeum building. All cars were drawn by horses until 1853.

It was this railroad that was part of the greatest fire Troy ever had in 1862 when their bridge over the river caught fire from sparks from an idling train and burned down most of downtown Troy, some 500 buildings were lost up to 8th Street.

Cannon founded a rolling mill in early 1846 known as La Grand Cannon & Co on a meadow south of the furnace of Johnson & Cox, which built the Clinton Foundry (stove makers) between Madison and Monroe Streets. Between them they had about 300 men. Cannon eventually

All cars of the Rensselaer and Saratoga Railroad were drawn buy horses until 1853. The Troy House is now Senior Citizen apartments. From Weiss; History of Troy.

Cannon's rolling mill eventually became part of Ludlow Valve which burned in the 1970s. Photo by LOC.

sold his interests to John A. Griswold & Co and were known as the Rensselaer Iron Works. They consolidated with the Albany Ironworks in March 1875 and became known as the Albany and Rennselaer Iron and Steel Company. Erastus Corning was president. The Rensselaer Rolling Mill made rivets and other items for the USS *Monitor* during the Civil War. The site later became Ludlow Valve. One main building burned in the 1970s. The last remaining building burned a couple of years ago and was directly across from the old Bruno Machinery complex.

Cannon was also a director of the New York and Albany RR Company, had a steamboat named for him, and Cannonsburg was founded in Kent County Michigan on a branch of the Grand River, 7 miles north of Ada Station on the Detroit & Milwaukee RR, 150 miles from Detroit. The village was made on December 1, 1848, for Le Grand Cannon on his behalf. He had to give it up in 1852 because his agent, E. B. Bostwick, failed to pay taxes on it and the land was first settled in 1837.

Lot 130 and 131 were sold to William H. Frear on May 4, 1891. He paid Le Grand Cannon, $124,000 for it. Frear began his business career on March 1, 1859, as a salesman for a dry goods store owned by John Flagg, 12 Fulton Street, in the Boardman Building. He took on a partner, Sylvanus Haverly on Feb. 11th, 1865 as Haverly & Frear on March 9th in the sale of dry goods on 322 River Street, between Fulton and Grand Division Streets. Another partner John Flagg was added on March 16,

The Anthenamum Building. Now parking lot across from number 9 First St.

Flag & Frear (1869-1874) advertising their products at the County Fair.

1868, and was known as Flagg, Haverly & Frear and they moved into 3 and 4 Cannon Place on April 9, 1868, basically taking over the previous occupants Decker & Rice, also a dry goods and millinery store. Haverly left on January 2, 1869, and Flag left on March 1, 1874, leaving the firm to Frear.

Le Grand B. Cannon, son of Cannon Building founder. From his report on the battle of the USS Monitor, which his father helped build.

Le Grand's son Leland Bouton Cannon was born in NYC on Nov 1, 1815. He went to RPI and graduated in 1834 and worked first for his dad's iron mill and at 19 worked in a wholesale dry goods store for 12 years. He then returned to NYC and also had an estate in Burlington Vermont known as Overlake (destroyed by the family in 1925) overlooking Lake Champlain. He retired in 1854 and reorganized the Whitehall and Saratoga Railroad and later became interested in the Champlain Transportation Company. He became VP of the Delaware and Hudson Canal Company when it took over the Champlain Transportation Company. He also was president of the Lake George Steamboat Company and

USS Monitor. Hull plates were made in Troy.

Crown Point Iron Company and was a director in numerous banks and companies. He became a congressman in the 8th congressional district of NY in 1866 as a Republican. In 1838 he was an aide to General John E. Wool of Troy. He was Wool's aide-de-camp and chief of staff as a colonel at Fortress Monroe during the Civil War and the famous battle between the USS Monitor and Virginia (Merrimac). He wrote a report on the condition of slaves who fled to the federal lines that were adopted and carried out in orders effectively emancipating former slaves employed by the army nine months before the emancipation proclamation. As a witness of the battle of the Monitor and Virginia, he wrote a report about the event for the US Navy Department. You can read it here:

https://catalog.hathitrust.org/Record/008727616

The fire of 1862 was caused by the burning of the Rensselaer and Saratoga Railroad Bridge.

He purchased the ruins of Fort St. Frederick on Lake Champlain and restored them. He died at the age of 91 in 1906.

In 1970 the Cannon Building was listed on the National Register of Historic Places. It is also a contributing property to the Central Troy Historic District, listed on the Register in 1986. A few years ago, movie producer and developer Sandy Horowitz purchased the building and turned it into a successful extended stay hotel using its original name, Cannon Place. It continues to also house smaller businesses on the first and upper floors making the Cannon Building one of the oldest continually operating commercial buildings in the United States.

UPDATE. It is now being converted to apartments.

Cannon Building in 2021. Photo by Kenneth C. Zirkel under Cretiave Commons License.

Will The Real Uncle Sam Stand Up!

First published on November 10, 2013, at 2:32 AM

It seems some writers are all fired up that Troy, NY claims to be the home of "Uncle Sam" via the life of Samuel Wilson who lived in Troy from the late 1700s to 1854. These writers point to this publication or that publication to try and prove that the term Uncle Sam was used to denote the United States before Samuel Wilson's connection. Let's examine the issue and try to put this to rest.

Samuel and his brother Ebeneezer Wilson walked from Mason, New Hampshire to Troy in 1789 and it is written set up a brick-making business near the west side of Mt. Ida near Sixth Avenue and Ferry Street. It has been written that they supplied bricks for the first brick house to be built in the village on Second and Albany (Broadway) Streets and the two-story building was built for James Spencer. They made bricks also for the first courthouse and jail.

We do know that the Wilson brothers were involved in politics early on because on March 20, 1804, they were elected to a committee to elect Republican candidates. We know that Sam was involved in politics most of his life either serving on committees or being appointed to the position of inspectors of beef and pork in Rensselaer County and its towns by various governors. For example, on March 17, 1815, he was appointed inspector of beef and pork for Hoosick while Ebeneezer was appointed Justice of the Peace in Troy. On March 12, 1822, Sam was appointed inspector of beef and pork for the county of Rensselaer by Gov. De Witt Clinton. On March

Advertisement for Wilson's store and slaughterhouse in 1810.

Uncle Sam Wilson home at 144 Ferry Street. Torn down during the country's Bicentennial.

18, 1828, he was elected inspector of beef and pork in Rensselaer County with three others. The following year on July 14, 1829, he was president of the political committee dinner in Mechanic Hall and the following year 1830 the governor appointed him inspector of beef and pork for Rensselaer County. On Nov 10, 1835, Sam was president of a vigilance committee for the first four wards of the city. On November 10, 1837, he was elected president of a committee supporting Van Buren for Governor. On August 7, 1840, Samuel Wilson was nominated as president of the Democratic Committee at Military Hall, Rally of the Democracy of Troy, supporting Martin Van Buren. On August 11, 1840, he changed his mind apparently and wrote a letter to the editor of a newspaper stating he is dropping from the Whig party which supported Harrison but seems to have changed his preference back for Van Buren.

Sam Wilson was also known to own real estate around the state. He purchased and sold real estate in the Catskills with his younger brother Nathaniel and lived in Catskill for five years between 1817-1822. Ironically, Sam and Nathaniel lived in a house on Main Street that was the same house where Martin Van Buren married his bride in

Thomas Nast First Uncle Sam depiction 1869 carving turkey.

1807. He came back to Troy later in 1822. Nathaniel stayed in Catskills and died there in 1854.

So it is clear that before and after Samuel Wilson was attributed as the Government icon of "Uncle Sam" he was a well-known entity around New York State and beyond from his land holdings and political connections.

The Wilson's also were in the meat slaughtering business and general provisions which bought and sold produce and products from around the northeast. It is known that in the earlier days of Lansingburgh to the north the Northern Turnpike connected our region with the Vermont economic communities and provided a good back and forth flow of goods. Ebeneezer and Sam along with one of his in-laws James Mann (Sam married Betsy Mann) opened a dry goods crockery and grocery store known as Wilson, Mann & Co near the upper Ferry and opposite Ashley's old Stand (Ferry and River) in 1810. Sam also ran a store at Spring and Hill Streets near the Poestenkill. We know this business and the meat slaughtering business was in operation in 1810. Wilson's notoriety in politics, business, land holdings, and the slaughterhouse would have been known to Vermonters, those in neighboring Massachusetts, and elsewhere where the communities were connected by turnpike or rivers. Samuel Wilson had three homes in Troy, the first was at the site of the Plum Memorial Building on Ferry and Second. The second was destroyed to make room for the Russel Sage College Administration Building and the third was at 144 Ferry Street torn down during the country's Bicentennial Celebration in 1976. There was an attempt in the 1950s to get Congress to declare it a national monument but it failed.

What other writers have been lacking is the knowledge that if you grow up in Troy you know calling someone uncle or aunt was a very common way to acknowledge a friend of your parents or endearment to someone you knew. I had an Aunt Maybell and Aunt Stacia on Eight Street and 3rd Street. They weren't related to me but that is what I called them as a term of endearment and respect and I would bet money that any Trojan older than 50 will tell a similar story.

So we know that Sam Wilson, or "Uncle Sam" as he would be called by locals who knew him and liked him was a well-known politician and businessman in Troy BEFORE the War of 1812 and his reputation would have extended outside the immediate area and into regions of the Northeast in which he probably had business dealings.

His associations with the government then, well known already, were increased when he won the contract to supply meat for the War of 1812 to the troops that were stationed nearby in Greenbush. The soldiers called it "Uncle Sam's Beef." It's been written that a contractor for the army in the New Orleans district wrote asking for a supply of beef and insisted it had to be the "Uncle Sam brand." It is here where the story was told about the connection. And the newspaper connects Uncle Sam to Sam Wilson as early as 1813.

Now some deriders claim that there were other suggestions as to the use of U.S. – Uncle Sam and not with Sam Wilson. However, these references are all after the 1812 connection to Sam Wilson.

The Troy Post wrote in its September 7, 1813 edition:

"Loss upon loss, and no ill luck stirring [sic] but what lights upon Uncle Sam's shoulders, exclaim the Government editors....This cant name for our Government has got almost as current as "John Bull." The letters U.S. on the Government waggons, & C., are supposed to have given rise to it."

Key phrase here is *"waggons & C.,* "which means other things too like perhaps barrels of meat, and of course, the barrels were all moved in wagons? So is the comment referring to the U.S. on the wagons or the barrels in the wagons or both? We already know that the U.S. on barrels was attributed to Wilson. So this statement does not disprove the Wilson connection at all but being written in Troy where the term originated makes perfect sense in print. It is important to point out that the majority of the printed accounts of Uncle Sam and Samuel Wilson were all local and regional Northeast newspapers.

The February 3, 1814 edition of the Commercial Advertiser states:
"Herkimer Jan 27. "Uncle Sam's hard bargains – on Thursday afternoon of last week, about thirty sleighs, "more or less" loaded with the "weak and wounded, sick and sore" of our armies on the frontiers, passed through this village for Greenbush."

Since Sam Wilson was connected to the barracks at Greenbush as the meat supplier this entry does not dispute the Wilson connection at all.

The Aug 12, 1816, New York Courier wrote:

"Uncle Sam's Pedigree.
Uncle Sam is a cant phrase, significant of the United States; as John Bull signifies England. The origin of it seems [my emphasis] *to be this. In the year 1807, there was authorized by law, the raising of a regiment of Light Dragoons. That initial letters USLD were painted on their caps, meaning the United States Light Dragoons. A countryman seeing a regiment of them passing by, inquired of a bye stander what they were and received for answer "They are Uncle Sam's Lazy Dog's don't you see it on their caps!" This story soon got amongst the soldiers and they have ever since denominated the United States "Uncle Sam."*

The problem with this entry is twofold. First, it says the origins *seem* to be this? And it also does not say when the so-called bystander answered? Did he see the regiment passing by in 1807 or 1816? Probably the latter and Sam Wilson was already established as Uncle Sam so the USLD falls right in line with what the troops were already associating the U.S. with Sam Wilson.

On Aug 14, 1817, The Northern Post citing the local Albany Gazette wrote:

"Uncle Sam"
This expression, which originated, during the war, from the initials US on the soldier's knapsacks, has come into general use. The indians at the west, from hearing it often used have imbibed the idea

Jack and Kevin Rittner at the Uncle Sam Gravesite in Oakwood Cemetery. Photo by Don Rittner.

that it is actually the name of the president; and while at Sacketts Harbor, a considerable number of indians and squaws, crowded round the president, wishing as they expressed it, "to shake hands with Uncle Sam."

Again, they state that the expression came into use during the war but Sam Wilson was already associated with the U.S., so the knapsacks having US on them could still be easily associated with Sam Wilson. The initials were already associated with Wilson in 1813 four years before this posting.

The Troy Daily Times published this Obit on July 1, 1854:

"Died – Samuel Wilson, aged 88 years, died this morning at his residence, 76 Ferry Street. The deceased was one of the oldest inhabitants of this city. He came to Troy about the year 1793 and consequently had resided here sixty-one years. He was the last of those termed "First settlers." Mr. W. purchased the lands east of this city, now owned by Messrs. Vail and Warren, and occupied by them for farming purposes till about 1820. He then sold them all, except four acres, upon which his present residence stands. He has been one of the most active business men of the community, and we can truly say he was an honest and upright man."

When Wilson died in 1854 at his home at 144 Ferry Street the Albany Evening Journal paper published this Obit on Aug 2:

"Uncle Sam
The death of Samuel Wilson, an age, worthy and formerly enterprising citizen of troy, will remind those who were familiar with incidents of the War of 1812, of the origin of the popular soubriquet for the "United States."

Mr. Wilson, who was an extensive Packer, had the contract for supply in the northern army with beef and port. He was everywhere known and spoke of as "Uncle Sam:" and the "U.S" branded on the heads of Barrels for the army were at first taken to be the initials of "Uncle Sam" Wilson, but finally lost their local significance and became through the army, the familiar term for "United

States." The Wilson were amongst the earliest and most active citizens of Troy. "Uncle Sam", who died yesterday, was 84 years old."

What is important in this obit is the phrase, *"he was everywhere known and spoke of as Uncle Sam."* This obit was picked up by many newspapers and republished. No one ever wrote a rebuttal to it.

One writer remarked that why did the Troy Post obit not mention the Uncle Sam connection? Pretty easy. Between 1812 and 1854 there were 35 newspapers published in Troy. Do you think every obit writer knew the complete history of everyone who died there? The fact that the Albany editor knew it just proves the point.

The New York Herald Tribune on June 12, 1889, quoting the Chicago News wrote:

"How 'Uncle Sam' Got his Name
The term came into use in the War of 1812 and originated in Troy, N.Y. The Government inspector there was Samuel Wilson, universally known as Uncle Sam. Whenever he inspected supplies furnished the Government he would brand them U.S., meaning United States, but the abbreviation, being then new and not generally recognized, the workmen supposed it to mean Uncle Sam, the inspector. Afterward, the story was repeated and got into print, and from that time the name has been facetiously applied to the United States."

The Red Hook Journal on January 13, 1892, published this:

"At the beginning of this century the slaughtering of cattle and packing of beef for New york, Boston, and Philadelphia markets was pursued as a business by the first of Ebeneezer and Samuel Wilson, two brothers from Mason, N.H. who had settled at Troy in 1789. At their two large slaughter houses they frequently killed 1,000 head of cattle weekly for shipment to those cities. When the war of 1812-15 began their beef and pork were in great demand and not a few army contractors gave them large orders for the delivery of these meats packed in barrels at a certain places where the army was encamped. From time to time their contracts stipulated for the delivery of these provisions at the camp at Greenbush, where, among other recruits, were a number from Troy.

The soldiers from Troy, seeing the barrels of beef and port marked with the letters "U.S." by the government inspectors, denominated them as "Uncle Sam" meaning that Samuel Wilson, whom they familiarly called "Uncle Sam" was the person from whom the meat was purchased. The other soldiers assuming that the term "Uncle Sam was applied to the letters U.S. Stamped on the barrels, began using the appellation "Uncle Sam" figuratively for the United States Government. From that time the designation "Uncle Sam" for the letters "U.S." grew into popular acceptance and has ever since been as familiarly known as that of "John Bull" for the English nation."

The Northern Christian Advocate in 1896 published the following:

"How "Uncle Sam' Got his Name
The nickname "Uncle Sam," as applied to the United States government, is said to have originated as follows: Samuel Wilson, commonly called "Uncle Sam" was as a government inspector of beef and pork at Troy, NY about 1812. A contractor, Elbert Anderson, purchased an quantity of provisions, and the barrels were marked "E.A", Anderson's initials , and U.S." for United States. The latter initials were not familiar to Wilson's workmen, who inquired what they meant. A facetious fellow answered, "I don't know, unless they mean "Uncle Sam." A vast amount of property afterward passed through Wilson's hands marked in the same manner and he was often joked upon the extent of his possessions. The joke spread through all the departments of the government, and before long the Unites States was popularly referred to as "Uncle Sam."

No one wrote a rebuttal to this publication or any of the others that attributed Sam Wilson as America's Uncle Sam.

Two years later the New York Herald published this:

"How Uncle Sam was Christened
The origin of the term "Uncle Sam" asked for by H.C.G, is kindly furnished by J.B. Franks. He says: "The term came into use during the War of 1812 and originated at Troy N.Y. The Government inspector there was Samuel Wilson, universally known as "Uncle Sam." Whenever he inspected supplies furnished the government he would brand them "U.S." meaning United States, but the abbreviation being then new and not generally recognized, the workmen supposed it to mean" Uncle Sam," the inspector.

Uncle Sam Monument in Troy.

Afterward the story was repeated and got into print and from that time the name has been facetiously applied to the United States."

No one wrote a rebuttal to this story.

Two years later the Irish Work and American industrial Liberator wrote on October 13, 1900 this:

"During the war of 1812 the United States Government employed an inspector by the name of Samuel Wilson. He was familiarly known as Uncle Sam. It was his duty to inspect the supplies furnished under contract by Elbert Anderson, and upon all goods that passed inspection, he marked the letters EA – US the initials of the contractor and the United States. Some wag suggested that the letters U.S. stood for Uncle Sam Wilson, and from that day to this the United States have been called Uncle Sam."

Only two years later the same paper would write:

"Uncle Sam"
The Wilson homestead, the birthplace of the original "Uncle Sam" was sold at auction April 30 for $1500. The purchase is Capt Orren A Hamblett, of Washington. "Uncle Sam" was Samuel Wilson, born on the farm. During the second war with England he and his brother Edward were contractors for government supplies at Troy, NY. It was the Wilson's idea to label their beef and pork barrels "U.S." and as Samuel Wilson was called "Uncle Sam" the army quickly referred to the supplies as "Uncle Sam's." This title quickly was applied to the government and after the war was used everywhere in that sense. Samuel Wilson died in Troy in 1854, age 88 years. The farm was sold because of the death of the last member of the family. It was owned by a Wilson for 122 years."

One of the best explanations appeared in the journal *American Notes and Queries* dated June 15, 1889.

"WHENCE THE NAME "UNCLE SAM"?

This familiar phrase is used as a cant designation of the United States Government, just as John Bull is made to represent the English nation, Johnny Crapaud, the French people, etc. The name is said to have originated in the following manner:

At the time of the War of Independence, there lived at Troy, N. Y., a man named Samuel Wilson, familiarly known to the inhabitants of that vicinity as Uncle Sam, who, together with Ebenezer, his brother, performed the duties of government inspector of the pork and beef purchased by the administration. Among others to purchase provisions for the army, came a certain Elbert Anderson of New York, who, having concluded a large contract, ordered the cases to be marked with his own initials, addressed to the United States.

It was the habit of Uncle Sam Wilson to superintend large shipments in person, and his appearance among the workmen in his employ was always the signal for an interchange of good-natured jocularities. On this occasion it fell to the lot of a facetious young Yankee to do the lettering on the cases containing the provisions; and he accordingly marked them all very carefully in white paint, with the letters "E. A.— U. S." Being interrogated by some of his fellow-workmen as to the significance of the initials (for at that time the abbreviation U. S. for United States was still a novelty), he replied that he did not know, unless it meant Elbert Anderson and Uncle Sam, meaning by the latter, his good-natured employer. This pleasantry occurring in the presence of "Uncle Sam" himself, "took" immediately among the workmen, who, repeating the joke in various forms on every subsequent purchase, were never weary of rallying him upon the rapidly increasing extent of his property.

Many of these same men, being staunch patriots, were shortly afterward numbered among the recruits, and pushed forward to the frontier lines, for the double purpose of meeting the enemy and of helping to devour the provisions they had labored to prepare. They carried with them their old jokes, especially their favorite story of "Uncle Sam"; and before the first campaign had ended, it made its first appearance in print. Spreading rapidly, and encountering universal recognition as "a good thing," the expression took firm root, and will doubtless continue to flourish as long as the government itself.

As the common personification of the U. S. Government, "Sam" became the popular synonym for the "Know-nothing" or "American" party, the controlling principles of which organization seem to have been a sublime ignorance in all matters concerning the inner workings of their society, combined with a general impression that "Americans must rule America."

The adoption of the letters U. S. on the knapsacks of the soldiers, gave rise to the well-known Americanism, "to stand 'Sam,'" meaning that the government of Uncle Sam must pay, or bear, the expenses of all those who wear his livery; and a song, current at that period, further developed this idea of dignified dependence, in its refrain, "Uncle Sam is rich enough to buy us all a farm." When Samuel Wilson, the "hero of a hundred "— tales, died at his home in Troy, in August, 1854, at the age of 84, the Albany Argus referred to and recalled the circumstances which had led to the adoption of his name as a sobriquet of the U. S.

In the cartoons of "Uncle Sam," frequently displayed in current illustrated newspapers, he is depicted as a tall, spare man, with a long, slim, straggling beard on his chin, attired in a dress-coat of blue, bespangled with white stars, and a pair of red and white striped trousers, fastened to his boots with straps; he has long outgrown his clothing, and the straps have stretched half way up his leg; on his head, at an angle perilous to safety, rests a white hat of cylindrical shape, known in vulgar parlance as a" stove-pipe "; a limp and generously expansive collar, confined by a loose redundancy of neckcloth, completes this figure of a typical Yankee.

Although in reality the prop and mainstay of a mighty nation, "Uncle Sam," when not engaged in offering some gallant service to the National Goddess, is generally represented as entirely absorbed in whittling a piece of wood. But this assumed indifference is deceptive. Let the British Lion be heard to roar never so timidly on the remotest confines of his territory, and Uncle Sam casts away his jack-knife in a trice, and stands ready to do doughty service for his country and his country's liberty."

Sam and Nathanial lived here at 251 West Main in Catskill from 1817 -1822. Catskill could save its one Uncle Sam house but Troy could not save three of them. Photo from the Internet.

In 1928 a representative in Indiana introduced a bill to make a Samuel Wilson buried in Merriam, Indiana the man behind the symbol of Uncle Sam. Jay Dunn a Troy Salesman read in a newspaper about the Indiana proposal and wrote to its congressman seeking to stop it. Trojans jumped right into action to disprove this and in 1931 the city of Troy wanted a memorial to him.

Lucius E. Wilson a great-grandnephew of Samuel wrote to the city explaining the connection and wrote:

"The landing of a party of visitors here at a wharf where the casks and barrels were assembled for shipment to Greenbush. One of the party asked who owned the provisions. The watchman is said to have replied.

"It is all marked, sir, and it all belongs to Mr. Anderson and Uncle Sam."
"Uncle Sam? Uncle Sam who?" the inquirer pursued.
"Why Uncle Sam Wilson," was the reply. "Don't you know? He owns all about here and is feeding the army."

That same year on May 16, 1931, the Uncle Sam monument and plaque were placed on Wilson's grave at Oakwood Cemetery. It was secretly paid for and arranged by Mrs. Marion Wilson Sheldon, the granddaughter of Sam Wilson. Later in 1961, she had a statement read by the Mayor at the time:

"As the granddaughter of Samuel Wilson and the last direct descendant bearing his name, I offer you greetings. Although unable to be with you at this time, I greatly rejoice that I have lived to see this glorious day, in which representatives of our grate Nation are gathered here to honor the memory of Samuel Wilson, that dear old man, whose deep love for his fellowmen, together with his upright characteristics won for him the name of "Uncle Sam" and the distinction of being the typical America. Not only in a humorous way, but also with deep respect does he impersonate our great Republic at home and abroad.

Uncle Sam is known to young and old, to friend and foe, as the straightforward honest character, typifying the vigorous American spirit everywhere. His army guards our homes; his Navy ploughs the seas. In the hearts of the people he ranks above potentates ad Presidents. With his lank body clad in star spangled hat, tight garters and coast as brilliant and brave as the America Flag, his image on the printed page represents at a glance all this is American, depicting Truth and the real America Spirit much better than any written word.

Underneath his rough rock, so typical of his rugged charter, lie the physical remains of Uncle Sam but his all-embracing spirit you find wherever the Star Spangle Banner is waving.

Unaware of his contributions to hour history and heritage, Samuel Wilson passed away proving the truth of an old saying that: "A great man is he, who had done no great deed, and ye has become great."

We, who are Citizens of this Nation and therefore are all Uncle Sam's children, should not allow his name to remain unsung. As his granddaughter, I have, in my humble way, endeavored to commemorate his deeds, and to give to the present and the future Citizens of our glorious America an inspiration follow.

And now we leave him to his rest.
The loved ones lying her.
Our Nation wide in cheer"
Thanks, and God bless you all
Signed Mrs., Marion Wilson Sheldon."

Post Card of Uncle Sam from Troy NY and proud of it!

In 1952, Representatives Dean P. Taylor of Troy and Representative Leo W. O'Brien of Albany presented a bill to Congress to acquire 144 Ferry Street and make it a national shrine. It failed. The building was razed during the Bicentennial. But it was thanks to Jessie F. Wheeler in 1961, a retired librarian from the Troy Public Library and Mrs. Elizabeth Allen Thiessen of Troy that we even knew the Sam Wilson connection. Wheeler spent 40 years collecting material supporting the connection between Wilson of Troy and Uncle Sam. Mrs. Robert Wood Coe, great, great niece of Wilson testified to the Senate Judiciary Subcommittee on Jul 11, 1961, as to the Troy connection of Uncle Sam with Wilson. She retold about her grandmother Harriet Allen Jackson who lived in Massachusetts and often spoke about her great uncle. Her uncle William H. Jackson, the famous painter and photographer (who also lived and worked in Troy for a while) painted Uncle Sam but the family never released any of the pictures to the public.

So, to summarize. If it was good enough for the entire 19th-century press to give Sam Wilson credit – without anyone contradicting it, It's good enough for me. Those great words from his granddaughter acknowledging the Troy connection? Good enough for me! The fact that the U.S. Congress passed a law proclaiming September 13, 1989, "Uncle Sam Day," (the birthday of Troy's Samuel Wilson) is good enough for me! And finally, the Joint Resolution of September 15, 1961, that passed recognizing"Uncle Sam" Wilson, of Troy, New York, as the progenitor of America's national symbol of 'Uncle Sam,' is good enough for me!

I would say that there is enough evidence that Troy's Sam Wilson and America's Uncle Sam are the same entity.

For those who disagree? Get over it.

You Better Run For Your Life

First published on October 3, 2013 at 2:44 AM

According to the United States Geological Survey landslides constitute a major geologic hazard because they are widespread, occur in all 50 states and U.S. territories, and cause $1-2 billion in damages and more than 25 fatalities on average each year. The recent avalanche in Colorado that tragically killed a family is not common but has happened in the past locally as well. The city of Troy has had several serious landslides that have killed many people and destroyed homes and livestock, particularly during the 19th century.

Mt. Ida, or Prospect Park, also known as Warren's Park, is geologically speaking a delta formed when a stream emptied into the quiet body of Lake Albany when it covered most of the Hudson Valley some 15,000 years ago. Lake Albany silt and clay were deposited on that delta and from time to time have shifted. Most of Troy is built on top of these Lake Albany clay deposits. Historical building practices and adding in some places 30 feet of fill to the head of the slope added additional weight to an already unstable slope not to mention excavating fill from the slope bottom.

The most recent landslide in Troy was in 2011 when Hurricane Irene came through the area. Several homes were destroyed along Route 2 in the Mt. Ida neighborhood when part of these postglacial materials slid down from Highland Avenue to the bottom of Congress Street or Route 2.

The most disastrous landslides took place in the 19th century and the first landslide along Mt. Ida took place in July 1835 in a right line with Division, Liberty, and Washington Streets.

Workman was excavating the toe of the hill for sand and gravel for filing in

Glacial Lake Albany covered most of Troy and deposited great amounts of clay and silt. Source: NYS Geological Survey

the streets and a large meadow south of the city that was being laid out in city lots. While they were at dinner a quarter of an acre of clay from the top of Mt. Ida came crashing down missing four or five houses nearby. A few weeks later, at 10 AM, a stream of water began gushing in the area near the top of the bank, carrying sand and gravel down into Division and Liberty Streets. The noise from the rushing water could be heard half a mile away.

Several houses along Rt. 2 were destroyed by a landslide in Troy, N.Y. on Monday, Aug. 29, 2011. Hurricane Irene caused major damage and flooding in the Capital District. (Lori Van Buren / Times Union).

Troy is famous for its springs. Many Trojans even today tap that spring water from the popular location at Spring Avenue. Historically, there were springs at 9th street north of Hoosick, and the well-known Whalen Bottling Plant at Jefferson and Fifth during the 19th century supplied Troy spring water in clear raised lettered bottles for sale. Glacial meltwaters filled the large deposits of glacial till that cover Rensselear County to the east and this water finds its way to the Hudson via streams like the Poestenkill, Wyanstkill, Piscawenkill, and spring outlets.

On January 1, 1837, another slide occurred in the same area around 7 PM. Nearly 500 feet of clay tumbled down to the base of the hill but kept moving another 800 feet along with sand and water sweeping up two stables and three homes crushing them. The stables and houses were pushed 200 feet west into a hollow on the corner of Washington and Fourth Streets. It also buried two brick kilns owned by A. Cone that lit up the sky with the flames. The three homes were occupied by Mr. John Grace, Mrs. Sarah Leavensworth, and a Mrs. Warner; the latter not at home when it struck. At the Grace house, John (57) and his wife Hannah (40) were pulled out dead but a boy was taken out alive. Four of the Leavenworth household, Sarah, and three children were in her house. Two children, Isaac (8) and Seaman (4) were crushed to death. Mrs. Leavensworth survived and three others in her family were at church and missed the event. One son Amatus, 10, was missing and presumed dead. One daughter, Sarah and a grandson of John Grace, named John Cooly and his dog escaped with no injury. One of the stables owned by Mr. Bingham had 22 horses and nine or ten dirt carts. Only six horses survived. The clay was piled up 40 feet deep in some places.

On November 14th, 1840 another large portion came sliding down due to heavy rains and demolished a small house occupied by a family of "colored" persons. The next day a short distance south of the big slide took out an old barn. The hill south of the old avalanche had cracked along its whole surface and was in danger of coming down again. Just two days later another in the same spot brought with it an orchard that was on the side of the hill. No one was hurt.

Three years later a major slide caused considerable loss of life. On Tuesday, February 17, 1843, a slide took place in the same area as the one in 1837 around 3:30 or 4 in the afternoon. This time the hill came crashing down on nine homes and whole families were crushed to death with up to five or six feet of clay on top of them. Police, firemen, and citizens tried to pull people from the ruins. The buildings destroyed were newly built and full of workers who were renting them. This happened while twenty men were at the bottom of the hill bank carrying off the earth for months and

1881 Map showing Mt Ida and cluster of houses in the area of the recurring slides.

Mt. Ida Historic Slide Area.

narrowly missed death themselves. The owner of the land that was being dug had given a warning not to dig there fearing a slide but it was ignored.

The center of this slide was at Washington Street a little below what has been called the "five points" of the city (Liberty to Adams). The amount of blue clay slid 500 feet over a level area after it hit the bottom and stopped about 100 yards east of 5th Avenue (then Street) and was about 150 yards wide averaging 20 feet in depth. Two of the houses destroyed were on the east side of Fifth. The center of the slide was like the former; the head of Washington Street took the brut of the force on both sides with only one corner of Washington and Hill Streets being partially hit. A total of 8 houses in Washington were destroyed. It continued down Washington to Hill Street crossing a few yards then stopped.

The houses were owned by Daniel D. Day, a ship carpenter, Fifth Street below Washington; Robert Henry, a contractor, same location; Wm. Brazell, teamster, Washington, corner of Fifth; Wm. H Kilfoile, teamster, Washington; Zebulon P. Birdsdall, painter, Washington; William Purdy, Mason, corner of Hill and Washington, house partially destroyed, and Charles Dumbleton, 18 Hill Street.
Those that died were Mrs. Mathew (Margaret) Grennin (30) and son William (10 weeks); Mrs. William (Catherine) Brazell (26) and two children, Jane (4) and James (2);

Michael Dunn (28); Thomas Keely (Kelly) (40) and wife Elizabeth (30); Edward Dumbleton, a lad; a child of James Caldwell named John (4); two children of Daniel E. Day, David Jr (4) and an infant aged 8 weeks; Miss Ann Wilber (23); a child of Mrs. Gardner; Miss Jane Sanford (23), a total of 15. Ann Wilbur, sister-in-law of Mr. Birdsall actually escaped first but rushed to rescue the children and was then crushed. Also listed is a "teamster from the country."

Those that escaped alive were 31-year-old Mrs. Eliza Kilfoile, one arm broken; a child of Z.P. Birdsall; Jane McCollum; Mrs. Susan Gardner and her sister Maria Deniker, both were saved when falling timbers created conditions that prevented crushing; two children, not named; James Barnett and wife. A Mrs. Mary Dunn was missing and presumed under the clay but the elderly lady was found crowded into a space only big enough for a three-year-old. Her clenched hands buried in her face allowed her to breathe and was rescued. Mrs. Purdy grabbed her children to rush out the front door but down came the house and chimney, but the chimney left a hole that they could crawl out of and survive. A Mr. Underhill who was in charge of a garden and orchard on the hill next to the slide was alerted of the moving dirt under him by the snorting of his horses. He checked his horses and backed his team and only seconds later the road under which he was riding moments before roared down the hill. Rosa Johnson was found badly bruised and R. Pattison and four children made it but most injured in some way.

Birdsall and his wife were not home at the time leaving their children with a sister of the wife. One of the children and the sister of the wife were rescued alive. Two other children were found a few days later dead. One was named Walter S. Birdsall. Z. P. was an officer in an anti-slavery society. Also, his father was Major Benjamin Birdsall (1786-1818). While in command of the military station at Greenbush, he was shot and killed by one of his soldiers, a James Hamilton. The soldier suffered the death penalty for the crime according to ancestry.com.

Nine bodies were recovered in the first hour with five dead, one partly hurt, and three saved. A man with his team of horses was driving by and had to jump for safety but the horse and load of wood he was carrying were buried.

In total 18 were believed killed with 16 bodies recovered with a property damage estimate of $6825.

On February 23 another slide occurred but was not as big and was south of the large one. A woodshed was destroyed but a house was saved. Two large holes with water gushing were created along with a large chasm. The rest of the hill was described as a "hogs back." It was predicted that the hill slide would be leveled down to Washington Park where no buildings had been built yet.

Then on February 27 another slide south of the previous two occurred again with no loss of life. To make matters worse, Joseph J. Finkle of Brunswick decided to ride into the city on March 4th to survey the landslide that had taken place and when he returned to his team of horses that were parked in front of a store, he found them stolen. He found them later at the bottom of Congress near River Street.

The destruction of St. Peter's College.

Another avalanche struck Troy on April 11, 1846, at 2 PM not far from the others and two men were instantly killed along with a pair of horses. Again laborers were digging on the hill and probably caused it. The two that were killed ran but stopped to look back. Not a good idea.

It would take another 13 years for another slide to occur but it did at 8 PM on Thursday, March 17, 1859. This time it took out a building that was just being constructed as St. Peter's College at the head of Washington Street. It was being built on a large plateau just above a few houses on Washington and was going to be sizable at 200 feet long and five stories tall with two towers. Two stories were completed at the time Mt. Ida decided to deposit about 30 feet of clay into the rear of the building. The back wall slowed the progress a bit and then the built-up pressure continued to demolish the beams, walls, partitions, and much of the front wall. Fortunate none of the 100 people working on the building were there since they were all celebrating St Patrick's Day the day before but 20 minutes before the slide several kids were playing in the building. Fortunately, the building stopped the slide and prevented the loss of life since there was a hospital not far down from the building site.

While natural slides do occur it seems that these slides were manmade as almost each time workers were removing clay and sand from the base of the hill making it unstable. Much of this material was being used to fill up the lots near Washington Park and the streets there were raised five to 12 feet above the original surface to accommodate the lots. So as 20 acres of land were being filled in, two brickyards along the base of the hill were also excavating clay from Mt. Ida to make bricks and so the slides began. As one newspaper account put it, *"The Trojans will probably be visited with these disasters as long as they persist in digging away the base of Mt. Ida and then building under the bank they have undermined. Mount Ida has no more natural disposition to fall than other mountains, and it seems strange that they keep bringing it down on themselves after such repeated warnings."* This slide however was blamed on a spring that had found its way out of the clay banks and penetrated between the clay and sand making it slippery.

Eliza Kilfoile grave who survived the landslide in 1843. Photo by Christopher Phillippo.

Finally in 1890 during the Spring a slide took out several houses and killed three people and then on Sept. 17 another slide on Mt. Ida, then called Warren's Hill, came rolling down but no one was hurt. It was blamed on the heavy rains.

Until the 2011 slide on Congress, Mt, Ida has been relatively quiet, slide-wise. Let's hope it continues that way.

Christopher Philippo who has spent a great deal of research on this subject (and sends it to me regularly) found the following headstone in memory of one family who was a victim of the 1843 slide. It appears that there was some form of litigation going on in 1891 probably over the 1890 slide.

"The trial in the circuit court this week of an action growing out of the recent landslide on Mount Ida has revived memories of former landslides in that vicinity. In a secluded spot in Mount Ida Cemetery, near the stone bridge, there lies a fallen tombstone, the existence of which had been forgotten by even the custodian of the cemetery. This tombstone was erected as a memorial to two victims of the landslide of 1843. The inscription is now barely decipherable but reads as follows, the words being graven under a cross and two urns:

"This small testimonial of friendly gratitude is placed here by Christopher Heffernan in memory of his brother-in-law, Thomas Keeley, and wife Elizabeth, who fell victims to the avalanche on Mount Ida on the 17th February 1843. The former died in the fortieth year of his age and the latter in her thirtieth year. They were natives of Ireland, the county of West Meath. Requiescant in pace.   I. MURPHY."

Troy Daily Times. May 30, 1891: 5 col 3.

That once loved form is now cold & dead.
Each mournful thought employs;
And nature weeps her comforts fled,
And withered all her joys.

Hope looks beyond the bounds of time,
W[hen what we now deplore]
[Shall rise in full imm]**ortal prime**
[And bloom to fade] **no more.**

[But cease, fond nature,] **cease thy tears**
[Religion points on] **high;**
[There everlasting sp]**ring appears,**
[And joys that ca]**nnot die.**

Christopher informs me this is an old hymn on the death of a child that dates back to at least 1811.

You Must Be Nuts To Write A Dictionary?

First published on November 6, 2013, at 9:38 PM

The Oxford English Dictionary (OED) is recognized as the largest English dictionary in the world and began as a project to collect the language under one roof back in 1857. It would take another 27 years before it began publishing under the name *A New English Dictionary on Historical Principles; Founded Mainly on the Materials Collected by The Philological Society*.

The project began by Richard Chenevix Trench, Herbert Coleridge, and Frederick Furnivall, intellectuals from The London Philological Society, and today it is the oldest organization in the world dedicated to the study of language.

After a few starts and stops with editors, it finally got underway in earnest with the appointment of Sir James Augustus Henry Murray (February 7, 1837 – July 26, 1915), a Scottish lexicographer and philologist, as editor, and in 1878 the Oxford University Press agreed to publish it when finished.

James Murray, editor of the OED and colleague of Hall and Minor. Source, Internet.

Murray had many people assist in preparing the dictionary from all over the world but there were two American men whom Murray thanked in his preface that deserved special acknowledgments and were considered two of the most important contributors – Fitzedward Hall and Dr. William Chester Minor. Murray invited all of the major contributors to dinner in Oxford on Tuesday, October 12, 1897, to celebrate. Many remarks were made that night about Hall and Minor but they never showed up. Both were American. Both spent time in India. Both were soldiers. Both were a little nuts. Hall was from Troy.

Murray wrote in the preface of the dictionary's first volume: *"Still warmer acknowledgments are due to those gentlemen who, not occasionally, or for special words, but systematically and continuously, have read the proofs, to improve the work as a whole by criticism, or to enrich it by additions. And first of all, and above all others, to Mr. Fitzedward Hall, D.D.L., who, as a voluntary and gratuitous service to the history of the English Language, has devoted four hours daily to a critical examination of the proof-sheets, and the filling up of deficiencies, whether in the vocabulary of the quotation. Those who are familiar with these pages of his Modern English, his English Adjectives in-able, and his numerous articles and papers on special points of English, know with what an amazing wealth of evidence the author illustrates the history of every word, idiom, or grammatical usage, upon which he touches; the whole of his stick of quotations, references, and indices, he has generously placed at the service of the Dictionary, and there is scarcely a page to which he has not added earlier instances of words or senses than those which our Readers had found; many rare words and rare senses have been added entirely from his stores."*

William Chester Minor. Source: Internet

He also wrote about Minor: *"also the unflagging services of Dr. W. C. Minor, which have week by week supplied additional quotations for the words actually preparing for press;"* and *"Second only to the contributions of Dr. Fitzedward Hall;"* and *"in enhancing our illustration of the literary history of individual words, phrases and constructions, have been those of Dr. W. C. Minor, received week by week."*

Fitzedward Hall (March 21, 1825 – February 1, 1901), is better known as an American Orientalist and was born in Troy, New York in 1825, the son of Daniel Hall. He attended Rensselaer Polytechnic Institute (RPI) in 1842 and graduated with a degree in civil engineering. He then entered Harvard in 1846 but left before graduation in pursuit of a runaway brother in India at the insistence of his family. I'm not sure if he found his brother but he stayed in India after his ship wrecked in the Bay of Bengal and became a tutor in 1850, later a professor of Sanskrit and English at the government college at Benares, and while there narrowly escaped being killed by the explosion of a fleet of thirty boats laden with one hundred and eighteen tons of gunpowder. In 1855 he became inspector of public instruction in Ajmere-Merwara and then the Central Provinces a year later. In 1857 he fought as a rifleman for the British during the Sepoy Mutiny.

In 1860 he left India and moved to England as chair of Sanskrit, Hindustani and Indian jurisprudence in King's College London then to the library of the Indian Office. He was the first American to edit Sanskrit the "Vishnu Purana" and published several works from 1852 to 1880, but was fired from the India Office in 1869 when he was accused of being a foreign spy and an alcoholic. He also lost his membership in the Philological Society. He became a recluse, after fighting with many of his former colleagues, and moved to a small village in Suffolk, but continued to publish. He learned about the Oxford dictionary project and, even as a recluse, became one of the most important contributors by reading certain books for the use of certain words and then passing on those quotations to the editor. From Editor Murray's own preface Hall read for four hours a day on proofs and the rest of the time read for vocabulary. It has been written that at one time he submitted 200 examples of the use of the word "hand" but it had to be rejected since there want enough space for them all.

Murray wrote, "*When the Dictionary is finished, no man will have contributed to its illustrative wealth so much as Fitzedward Hall.*" They never met and Hall died at Marlesford, Suffolk, on February 1, 1901.

Dr. William C. Minor (June 1834 – March 26, 1920), the other American, was a whole other matter.

Minor was a 37-year-old surgeon from New Haven Connecticut but living in Lambeth, England when he killed a man who he thought was a member of the militant Fenian Brotherhood and who he thought was trying to break into his room. Minor had come to England a few months before after being in an insane asylum in the US and had retired from the army as Captain on grounds of being sick. An accomplished artist as well he brought his watercolors with him and eventually moved into Lambeth in 1871, an area that had easy access to prostitutes. It seemed that according to the army records he frequented the "Tenderloin Districts" as they were called everywhere he was stationed in the U.S. Having caught Gonorrhea a few times he even attempted to cure it by injecting white Rhine wine into his urethra – it didn't work. He was also afraid of the Irish and according to the doctor who was treating him, he was insane. He was found not guilty on grounds of insanity on April 6, 1872, and sentenced to the rest of his life in an asylum for the criminally insane in Broadmoor.

Murray did not understand why Minor didn't show up for the gala even though he was only 60 minutes away. That is until he decided to go visit his friend and colleague. Picked up by a coach and brought to a stately mansion Murray introduced himself to a person he thought was Minor after all these years:

"I, Sir, am Dr. James Murray of the London Philological Society, and editor of the Oxford English Dictionary. And you sir, must be Dr. William Minor. At long last. I am most deeply Honoured to meet you."

After a pause, the man replied:

"I regret not, sir. I cannot lay claim to that distinction. I am the Superintendent of the Broadmoor Criminal Lunatic Asylum. Dr. Minor is an American, and he is one of our longest-staying inmates. He committed a murder. He is quite insane."

Or so the story goes.

Yes, Minor had made all those contributions to the Oxford Dictionary while in an insane asylum all those years. The two scholars – Murray and Minor – did meet and became friends. When the other American Fitzedward Hall died Minor wrote a letter to Murray discussing his sadness for the former Trojan. On Dec 3, 1902, Minor cut off his penis while in his room at the asylum probably due to repentance to his earlier exploits with prostitutes and the newfound religion he had developed in his later years. After healing and a few other incidents, Winston Churchill signed his discharge papers and he returned home, an elderly, feeble man to an asylum in D.C. In 1919 he was released and spent the rest of his year on the Connecticut River in a Hartford retreat for the insane. He died there on March 26, 1920.

Murray had died earlier in 1915 and never saw the completed Oxford Dictionary. So it seems that the two most important contributors to the Oxford Dictionary were a bit on the crazy side. The Dictionary was published under the imposing name *A New English Dictionary on Historical Principles*. The original plan was a four-volume, 6,400-page work that would include all English language vocabulary from the Early Middle English period (1150 AD) onward. In the end, it contained over 400,000 words and phrases in ten volumes.

You needed to be insane to work on that project.

Troy Building Was Once An Early Printer And School

First published on May 22, 2013, at 6:58 PM

Looks like one of my favorite historic buildings in Troy may have a second life after all. I wrote about Number 9 First Street back in 2003 when it looked like it might get renovated but that project fell through. A new proposal now called "The Bindery" will convert it into a restaurant and lofts. We shall see.

The four-story brownstone and iron front building at number 9 First Street (originally numbers 8 & 9) is not only a historic building but was the home of a printing company that published Troy's earliest history books.

Built during the Civil War in 1864 by William H. Young, it features an ornate cast iron storefront cast by Starbuck Brothers Foundry formerly on Center Island.

Young's Building at 9 Front Street.

Today.

The Young Building showing Bryant & Stratton billboard along with Young's services ad, before 1875.

William H. Young was a bookbinder and bookseller and was born in Troy on November 3, 1817. His father James had come to Troy in 1796 to work as an apprentice to his cousin Colonel Nathaniel Adams, the leading gold and silversmith at the time.

On March 1, 1842, Young and Charles P. Hartt, a partner and old schoolmate, purchased the previous book and stationery business of Ebenezer Pratt who first began the business in the spring of 1821 on River Street opposite Titus's Tavern, not far from the present site. The First Street building also had an entrance on River Street, Number 214 that served as a storeroom.

During the mid-19th century, this section of First Street was known as Banker's Row; most of the buildings on the block were banks. In addition, the terminus for the Rensselaer and Saratoga Railroad was in a vacant lot and office building across the street from White's First Street entrance. The railroad office at 10 First Street and the location on the east side of the R&S RR Bridge (now the Green Island Bridge) was available from sunrise to 9 PM every day to take freight and people as far as Saratoga and stops between. The cars were horse-drawn until 1853.

In 1871, Young built a larger three-story building next door at 216 River and added a bookbindery and printing office.

Young is well known as the publisher of two of Troy's early histories by Arthur Weise, as well as many of the early city directories and other publications including religious and trade items.

Young also rented out the upper floors to a new business college called Bryant & Stratton Mercantile College, a firm originally from Ohio, and which later became

Fig. 40. (*top*) 1837 engraving of a lithography shop. The upper-story workshop is devoid of architectural embellishment.

Fig. 41. (*bottom*) 1865 advertisement for Bryant, Stratton & Folsom's commercial college, Troy, New York. Mercantile colleges training young men commonly rented quarters in the upper stories of buildings in the commercial district. Bryant, Stratton & Company was a large chain, with mercantile colleges throughout cities in the East and Midwest.

Inside classroom when it was the Bryant and Stratton Business School.

Bryant & Stratton & Folsom's Troy Business College. Bryant & Stratton Mercantile College was founded locally in Albany in 1857 and by 1865 they had a school in Troy, first at the Cannon Building later moving to number 9 First Street. B&S had a chain of about 50 schools at the time but split up in 1867 and each school took on its own name and life; the school in Albany became the Bryant & Stratton & Folsom's Albany Business College (ABC) and was owned by Ezekiel G. Folsom.

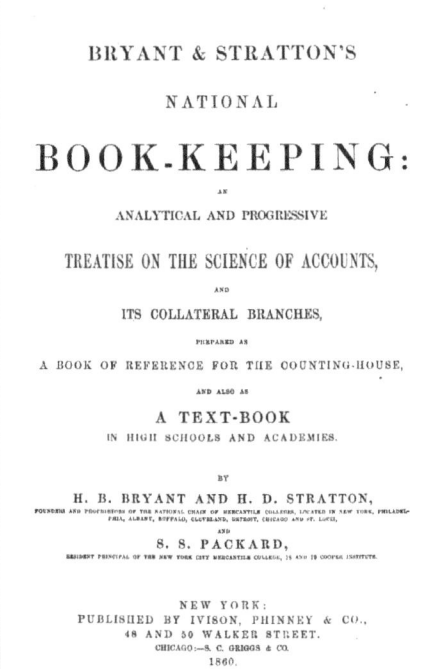

B&S published their own textbooks and were used in the Young building.

Book keeping class when it was Albany Business College.

Troy's earliest railroad depot was across the street from Young's building.

John Richard Carnell who purchased the Troy school in 1867 (Bryant & Stratton & Carnell) was born in Troy in 1845 and was a graduate of the Troy Business College in 1865. He also taught there. The school was incorporated in 1871 as the Troy Commercial College and moved to the Troy Times Building on Broadway and Third. Carnell sold it however in 1876 to Harrison B. McCreary and Thomas H. Shields. When the Times Building at the corner of Broadway and Third burned in February 1878, the college moved to Kennedy Hall at 13 Third Street.

Ironically both Bryant & Stratton and Albany Business College which were once owned by the same family (Folsom) merged in 1951. The Troy name was kept for years in hopes that it would be revived, but it never happened. In 1988, ABC was sold to Bryant & Stratton of Buffalo, and in 1989, the school was renamed Bryant & Stratton Business Institute and moved to its existing location on Central Avenue in Albany in 1990.

Unfortunately Number 9 First Street didn't fare so well and during its remaining years became a well-known flophouse. There is a certain amount of irony here. A "Young" entrepreneur who published histories of Troy built number 9 First Street in 1864 while a published poet lawyer built the adjacent Rice (Hall) building in 1875.

Let's hope that "The Bindery" project is successful as it will add one more great building back to Troy's continuing renaissance.

UPDATE. The building is now a popular eatery called Slidin' Dirty.

From Lindy's Alley To City Station

First published on November 9, 2012, at 11:26 AM

Cities, like humanity in general, slowly evolve ever so transforming, growing, and collectively changing the landscape on Earth. This is evidenced by the new development that is going on at Wilson's View, an area I named after Uncle Sam when I was a teenager and living on short 7th Avenue along Mt Ida. Sam Wilson's house was standing on Ferry Street not far from the Ahern Apartments where my Uncle Frank and Aunt Alma lived. My mother and I lived across the street at 1504 7th Avenue in a little two-story Federal-era home on the second floor. I often played with the kids that lived in Uncle Sam's house though names are forgotten now!

As Troy moved up the hill (Mt Ida) during the early 19th century the area that is now RPI's City Station, a complex of student residential and first-floor retail, consisted of

By the 1920s, Sixth Street between Congress and Ferry was known as Lindy's Alley after stable master Lindy Simon. Notice the railroad track control tower at the back of the picture. This was located just before the Union Depot and was used to switch tracks for upcoming trains. My father who worked at the station took me up and introduced me to the switchman. It was fascinating to see all the manual switches and lights on the board above them showing him which trains were on which tracks. Now done by computers. Photo by Keith Marvin.

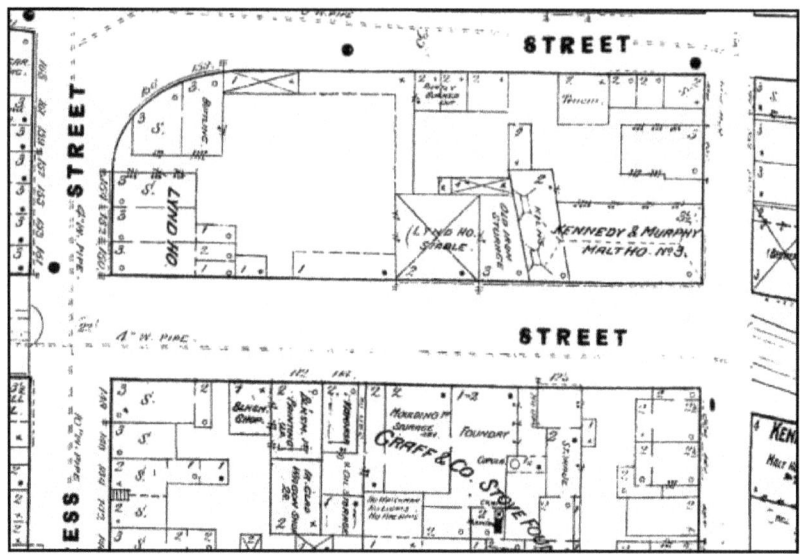
1885 Sanborn map showing 6th Avenue and development between the train tunnel.

a mix of housing, commercial and industrial businesses lining what was then called 6th Street, an unpaved short stretch between Congress and Ferry. The railroad tunnel for Union Station built in 1854 was created a few years earlier when they cut a trench through the Mount and built the arched tunnel between Ferry and Congress Streets covering it over with dirt. It is likely the time when that short stretch of pathway was populated with businesses. The tunnel was recently destroyed during the construction of City Station.

By the 1880s Wilson's View was the location for Graff & Company Stove Foundry, Kennedy & Murphy Brewery buildings, houses, and a grocery store owned by Cyrus Lynd. by 1900, the area mostly was populated with livery stables such as Westcott Express Company the largest and later replaced with Buchanan Baggage Transfer (The Union Depot train station was just down the street). Also, Sixth Street had been changed to Sixth Avenue.

By the roaring twenties, this short street became known as Lindy's Alley named after Lindy Simon who ran a livery and stable service there. The Tunnel Garage, Mack's Garage & Exchange, and Troy Bottle Exchange (milk bottles) were also popular businesses and a few residences rounded out the neighborhood.

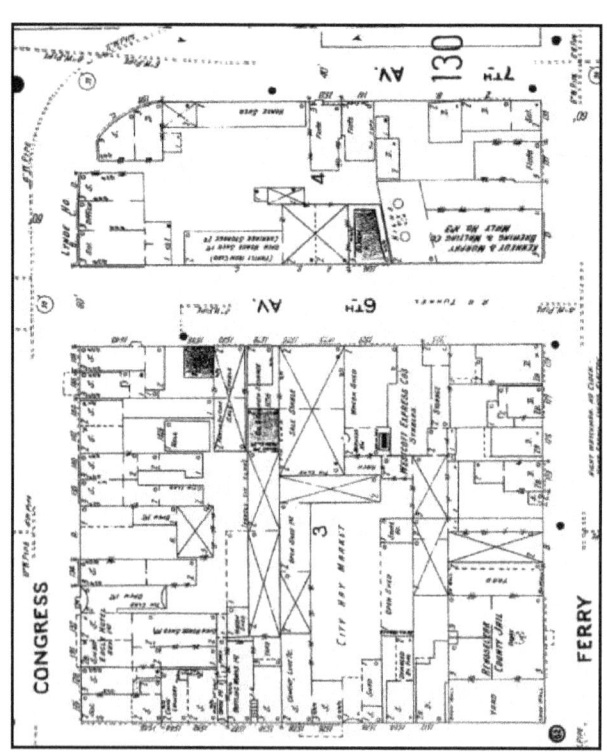
Sixth Avenue after the turn of the 20th century. Sanborn Map, 1903.

However, by the 1940s, post-war, there was a need for housing for all the returning war veterans and Lindy's Alley became the site for the John J. Ahern Apartments, a four-building complex that began construction in 1952 and finished in 1953. My Uncle Frank and his family moved into Building 1 between the tunnel and Short 7th. Later my mother moved to Short 7th in 1965. The tunnel area between the four buildings (two on each side) became parking and the recreation area for the kids that lived in the complex. I should

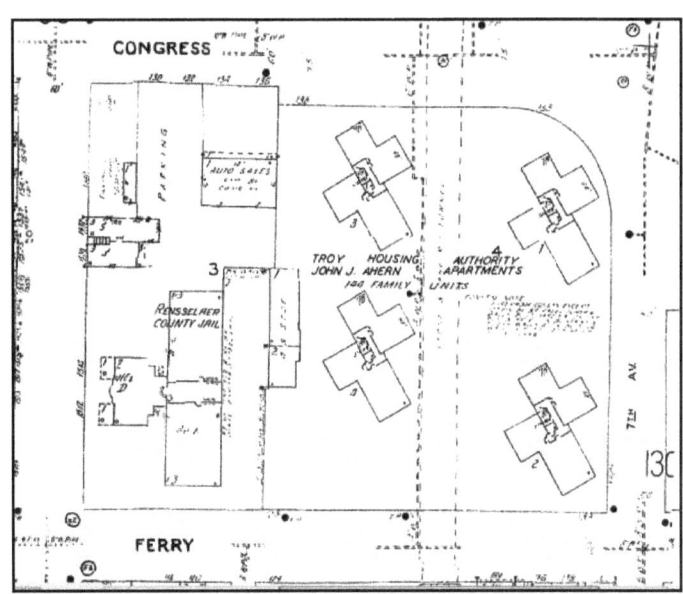

1955 Sanborn map showing the location of the Ahern Apartments and the tunnel.

Uncle Sam Wilson's house on Ferry and Short 7th Streets. The city tore it down during the country's Bicentennial in 1976. I use to play with the kids that lived there in the early 1960s.

Lindy's Alley on top of the tunnel, looking south from north of State Street.

point out that the recreation items included what only could be called concrete pipes and metal bars to climb. Lots of bumps on the head! The complex was named after the mayor of Troy, John J. Ahern (1944-47) who was reelected but died in 1950.

The Ahern Apartments became the homes of many of today's baby boomers and there are many good memories of the place. However in its later years, the complex became housing for low-income families, a drug haven, and eventually went the way of the wrecking ball in 2000 after failed attempts to sell them for renovation in 1992 and unsuccessful attempts to sell them for a Chinese cultural center and new public safety building for the city.

In the last couple of years, RPI has been building student housing calling the units City Station. Not sure where they came up with that name but once more that little stretch of road between Congress and Ferry will become an active community and that is not a bad thing.

Southbound NYC local to Albany exiting the tunnel on July 1957. You can see Lindy's Alley replaced by the Ahern Apartments parking lot and you can see the track switching tower in the background. Photo by Jim Shaughnessy. Only the retaining wall on the right remains. Looking North.

Lindy's Alley now. Photo by Don Rittner. Looking north.

Destruction of the tunnel in 2010 for no good reason. Looking south. Don Rittner.

For Whom The Bell Tolls?

First published on March 18, 2012, at 1:13 AM

Let's see if I have the facts right? The city of Watervliet is deciding whether to allow St Patrick's Church and surrounding buildings to be razed for a supermarket or some other box store? Hmm, a tough decision I'm sure? There are not enough supermarkets in the area and the Price Chopper three blocks away from there is not good enough, I guess?

The church? Well, it is only a replica of the Grotto of Lourdes Church in France and is one of the most impressive structures in the Capital District and can be seen for miles. The almost 150-foot bell tower is very special.

During the 19th and first half of the 20th century, Watervliet and Troy were world famous for making bells. There are thousands of them still ringing that have the name Meneely on them. The ring in Polynesia, Australia, Japan, China, India, Syria, Egypt, Africa, and just about any place in the world that has a religious structure.

There were two Meneely Bell companies – related by brothers – and they could see each other across the river. Clinton H. Meneely made the bells in Troy and Edwin and George ran the Watervliet foundry.

St. Patrick's Church in Watervliet today. Photo by Don Rittner.

It was in early January 1907 that one of the largest church bells in the world was inserted into the bell tower made by the Watervliet foundry. It was put into the tower at St. Patrick's!

The bell weighs a whopping 7,500

pounds made of 77% copper and 23% block tin and is a bit over 6 feet in diameter and 4 ½ feet tall. It rings in the key of Bb international pitch (bass clef). When hung with all the other connections it weighed in for a total of 11,000 pounds!

The bell was made as a gift from the Holy Name Society of the Parish and cost $3500. There are two inscriptions on it, one the name of the foundry and date and the other:

> In nomine Jesu genu
> Flectatur coelestium
> Terrestrium et infernorum
> Presented to
> St. Patrick's Church
> West Troy, Watervliet, N.Y.
> By the
> Holy Name Society
> George E. Hipwood, Prest.,
> Joseph T. Cavanaugh
> Francis Powers,
> Secretaries
> Thomas F., McLoughlin, Treas.
> Rev. W.F. Sheehan, M. R. Pastor

Our lady of Lourdes Grotto Church in France which St. Patrick's was modeled after. Photo from the Internet.

The Latin loosely translates to *"In The Name of Jesus, Should bow heavenly, Earth and of Hell."*

I realize that this is a tough decision for Watervliet and its citizens. The economy is terrible, small cities are struggling, and many are trying to do anything they can to bring in revenue. But unless this is a local Price Chopper being built we all know the profits made goes back to corporate headquarters in another galaxy. It does not stay here and the minimum wage jobs that go with the store do not make up for the eyesore that is left behind when the company decides it is no longer profitable and abandons it, leaving a cancerous scar in the city's landscape. How many examples in the Capital District do you want me to list?

I remember when Watervliet was a vibrant city with a downtown. Its downtown was indeed taken away by DOT when it built Interstate 787 and decimated the major retail area of the city. But continually allowing the building of anything just to try and build the tax base destroys the very fabric and character of the city and psychologically affects those that continue to live there.

The main street of Watervliet (19th St.) is starting to look like Anywhere USA. There is a vanilla box Rite Aid as soon as you exit the bridge from Troy, a Dunkin Doughnuts on the next block, and now a Shoprite or other big box store on the next block? Before too long you won't know if you are in Watervliet, Latham Circle, or Timbuktu?

Watervliet's 19th Street corridor is headed the same way as Hoosick in Troy. Just approve this development, the next one, and the next one, and then you have a complete mess. Continue to allow large-scale development like a drug store, supermarket, and other chains along that stretch, increase the vehicle traffic to get there, and soon after you will have a street that cannot handle the traffic. Then you will have to widen the street, create new peripherals streets, dump cars into once quiet neighborhoods, increase truck traffic for deliveries, and add new signal lights to try to regulate the traffic. You get the picture.

What may happen instead is those few travelers that do come into the city via the Troy Bridge on their way west will

How A Great Bell Takes Shape. The inside of core mold of the great 7,500-pound bell just completed and hung in the tower of St. Patrick's Church, Watervliet. Photo by F.F. Lotz, January 7, 1907. The Troy Times.

find other ways to go west (alternate Rt. 7) and the retail traffic will dwindle instead of increase. I avoid Hoosick like the Plaque. Just a thought!

It doesn't have to end this way. There are numerous examples of adaptive reuse of churches. I would suggest everyone read the 2004 MIT Dissertation *"Convert!: The adaptive reuse of Churches"* by Dennis Frenchman:

http://dspace.mit.edu/bitstream/handle/1721.1/35692/56409883.pdf?sequence=1

Frenchman uses a real successful case study of a pubic private Methodist church redevelopment in Plymouth, Mass, and in the appendix gives a list of many examples of church adaptive reuse. It is an excellent study and one all city planners should read. Of course, the best use of a church is as a church.

Illustration showing the casting or pouring of the big bell recently installed in the tower of St. Patrick's Church in Watervliet. Photo by F.F. Lotz, January 12, 1907. The Troy Times.

One of my favorite church adaptations is in Montreal. The Christ Church Cathedral is an Anglican Gothic Revival cathedral and is sitting on top of an underground shopping mall. It was declared a historical monument by the government of Quebec in 1988. In 1999 it was declared a National Historic Site of Canada.

Designed by Frank Willis and Thomas Scott the church opened in 1867. It went through some structural problems over the years but in the 1980s they decided to build a two-story mall UNDER the church to stabilize it. In 1987 the church was sitting on stilts, floating in the air, while they built the mall called *Promenades Cathédrale* which is quite a success.

There is good adaptive reuse in Schenectady where a Lutheran church is now the office of a graphic design firm. In Troy, there are plans to convert a church into

The other day this new great bell of sweet and dignified tone was hung in the tower of St. Patrick's Church Watervliet. Photo by F.F.Lotz, January 12, 1907. The Troy Times.

Condos. In Mechanicville, St. Luke's Episcopal Church has been converted to an arts center. It is also available for events like weddings and receptions. And if the Bishop hadn't pulled the rug out from under my feet in 1978 there would have been a city museum in a former church in downtown Albany. Yes, your holiness, I haven't forgotten after all these years!

Watervlieters will of course make their decision on what they want to do but it has to come a time when the residents of a community have to put their foot down and demand that developers do not have carte blanche

THE MENEELY BELL FOUNDERY.

At West Troy, N. Y. (opposite Troy). Established in 1826. Recently erected and enlarged brick structures have taken the place of the original buildings, which, with modern furnaces and other improved appliances, afford facilities for carrying on the Bell business unequaled either in extent or convenience. Twenty Thousand Bells have been made at this Establishment, including nearly one hundred Sets of Chimes and Peals — a product greater than that of all the other Founderies of the country combined. Connection with Troy by Bridge and Ferry; with Albany by Horse Cars and Railroad.

say in how they are going to destroy the fabric of a community to line their pockets. Developers develop to make money. They don't care if there is a special church, mansion, or archeological site in the way. It is their nature to build and that is not necessarily a bad thing. But if you let a kid in a candy store, there is bound to be collateral damage.

I am hoping that everyone can get together and come up with a plan that can prevent the demolition of St Patrick's.

Haven't we all had enough of this?

ADDENDUM on April 24, 2012

It appears that St. Patrick's had three Meneely Bells in its lifetime. This excerpt is from an 1876 Meneely Bell Catalog talking about a second bell:

> Rev. Wm. F. Sheehan, of West Troy, writes: "You know with what pride St. Patrick's congregation used to talk of the old Bell made by your father; how very much they regretted its loss, and the doubts expressed of your being able to supply its place. Will you be surprised when I tell you that we are more than delighted with the new Bell, and find it in every way superior to the old one. I am informed that it is looked upon at the Seminary (Provincial) as having the sweetest tone of any Bell in the vicinity."

Helen Finally Comes To Troy

First published on July 5, 2015, at 5:50 PM

ALERT: The first week of shows sold out. Tickets are still available for this weekend but selling fast.

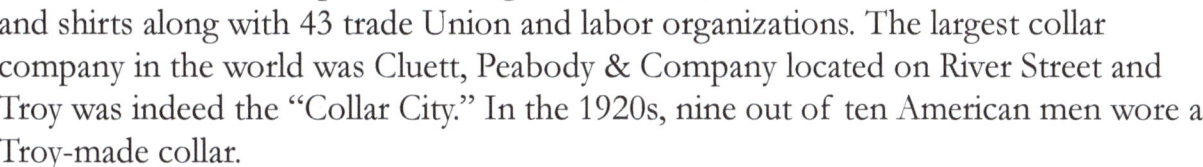

In 1923, more than 72.000 people lived in Troy, NY. Troy was the 98th largest city out of 282 in America and there were 30 companies making collars, cuffs, and shirts along with 43 trade Union and labor organizations. The largest collar company in the world was Cluett, Peabody & Company located on River Street and Troy was indeed the "Collar City." In the 1920s, nine out of ten American men wore a Troy-made collar.

The Arrow shirt with collar was also invented by Cluett-Peabody & Sons. In 1915, Frederick Forrest Peabody created a new advertising campaign to promote these shirts and hired the popular commercial artist, J.D. Leyendecker to come up with the famous Arrow Collar Man.

As a result, the Arrow Collar Man became the symbol of the perfect American male. By 1920 Leyendecker's ads, found in magazines in America and Canada, were a huge hit, and he became the male 'pin up' along with hundreds of marriage proposals from women up to the 1930s. Never mind the fact that Leyendecker was outwardly gay and his male models were often his lovers.

Due to this popularity, in 1920, J.C. McCarthy and H.C. Thorbahn published the hit song "My Arrow Collar Man." Also, Juliet Barker and H.C. Eldridge published another "My Arrow Collar Man," two years later.

So it is not surprising that a young upstart playwright by the name of George S. Kaufman would find the city of Troy and the Arrow collar along with the entire industry

Cluett, Peabody & Co was the world's largest collar and cuff maker. Image from the Internet.

fodder for a musical comedy.

In 1923, Kaufman and fellow playwright Marc Connelly wrote the two-act play *Helen of Troy, New York*. This play ran for three days at the premiere opening of the Fairmont Theater in Fairmont, West Virginia on June 4, 1923. Then to Broadway! The play appeared in New York City's Selwyn Theatre from June 19 to October 7, 1923, followed by a stint in the Times Square Theater from October 8, 1923, to December 1, for a total of 191 performances. George Jessel (yes, the comedian) produced the play and it launched the career of music writers Bert Kalmar and Harry Ruby. They later went on to write for the Marx Brothers movies, along with Kaufman. There were two directors, Bertram Harrison and Bert French. It was both Harrison's directorial debut and the second of only two plays for French. Harrison was known primarily as a producer/performer and French was famous as a choreographer/producer/designer and performer.

Joseph C. Leyendecker (1874-1951) was one of the country's premier illustrators and was responsible for the Arrow Collar Man that put Cluett, Peabody, & Co on Kaufman's radar. Image from the Net.

The play was a big hit and starred Helen Ford as *Helen of Troy*. Ironic, since Helen was born here in Troy on June 6, 1897, as Helen Isabel Barnett.

Helen never saw the light of day in Troy and my guess is the collar bosses wanted no part of it. They probably didn't appreciate getting poked fun at.

Kaufman went on to become America's leading dramatist with 45 plays, including the hits "The Man who came to Dinner," "Dinner at Eight," and

Former Cluett, Peabody & Co. Many of the buildings to the left were torn down. City Hall now rents in the former collar building. Image from the Net.

Joseph Leyendecker illustrated the Arrow Collar Man ad program and made the collars the most popular. Image from the Net.

others. He was an original member of the famed Algonquin Round Table and drama editor for the New York Times. He won two Pulitzer Prizes for drama that included the first ever for a musical. He also wrote for the Marx Brothers such hits as "A Night at the Opera," The Coconuts," and "Animal Crackers."

Like many plays, *Helen* faded into obscurity. It was of course written about a city at a time when Troy was important, the "big town," but like most of the

There were more women living in Troy than men in the early part of the 20th century due to the prevailing jobs in the collar industry. This is a picture of collar workers in Cluett, Peabody Co. Image from the Net.

industrial Northeast, the light doesn't shine so bright anymore. It is hard for the city to live up to the Collar City name. No collars are made here anymore. Cluett & Peabody, which at one time had eleven factories, left Troy in 1989 and now only the Arrow name survives and is owned by Philips-Van Heusen Corp., the same company that owns other name brands such as Calvin Klein and Tommy Hilfiger, for example.

Decades ago I found a copy of the Helen script at a local library and after reading it I was determined to have the play performed someday in Troy. As a historian, the play sheds some humorous light on a great era in American history – the 1920s. Kaufman, known for his wit, delivers some great one-liners, and while it is a comedy about Troy, he

The world's largest collar maker started small with George B. Cluett and brother. Image from Net.

Marc Connelly (1890-1980) co-wrote Helen with Kaufman. Image from Net.

New Hope, Pennsylvania — George S. Kaufman (1889-1961), Pulitzer-prize winning American playwright. Informal photograph of the author, near his residence in New Hope, Pennsylvania. — Image by © Bettmann/CORBIS

throws some barbs on larger issues of the time such as censorship. You have to be on your toes to catch it.

Finally, 82 years after opening in New York City and beginning July 9th and again on the 10th, 12th, 17th, 18th, and 19th, *Helen* will finally play in Troy at Fellowship Hall at 35 State Street. It's an early Bicentennial present to Troy. Next year Troy turns 200!

As serendipity would have it, I was introduced to Justyna Kostek, a young woman from Denmark (originally Poland) who was visiting America and who has her own theater company in Europe. She has directed many plays throughout Europe and was visiting America to see how American plays were produced and performed. I suggested to her the best way to see an American play produced was to codirect *Helen* with me. She agreed.

Helen Ford, born in Troy, played the lead Helen. Image from Net.

We put together a cast and team and you can see the results of this musical comedy for yourself. Seeing the costumes is worth the price of admission. We were lucky to get some great period clothes loaned to us by local Vintage shops Aurora's Boutique (Troy) and 72 Pearls (Denise Poutre, Albany) and individuals Sarah Fish and Phil Sawyer. If you like the costumes you can buy most of them after the show run. Just let us know.

We had a pianist accompanied by James Skelton on guitar. Olga N. Bogdanova, a professional dancer did the choreography (and plays two roles). Many of the show's original music has been lost over the years but I was able to recover seven of the thirteen original full arrangements.

Queenie Smith who played Maribel stole the show.

Unlike many plays, there are a lot of twists and turns in Helen besides the fact that Helen Ford played Helen of Troy. We wanted to perform in Troy – after all, it is about Troy – but could not find a suitable place.

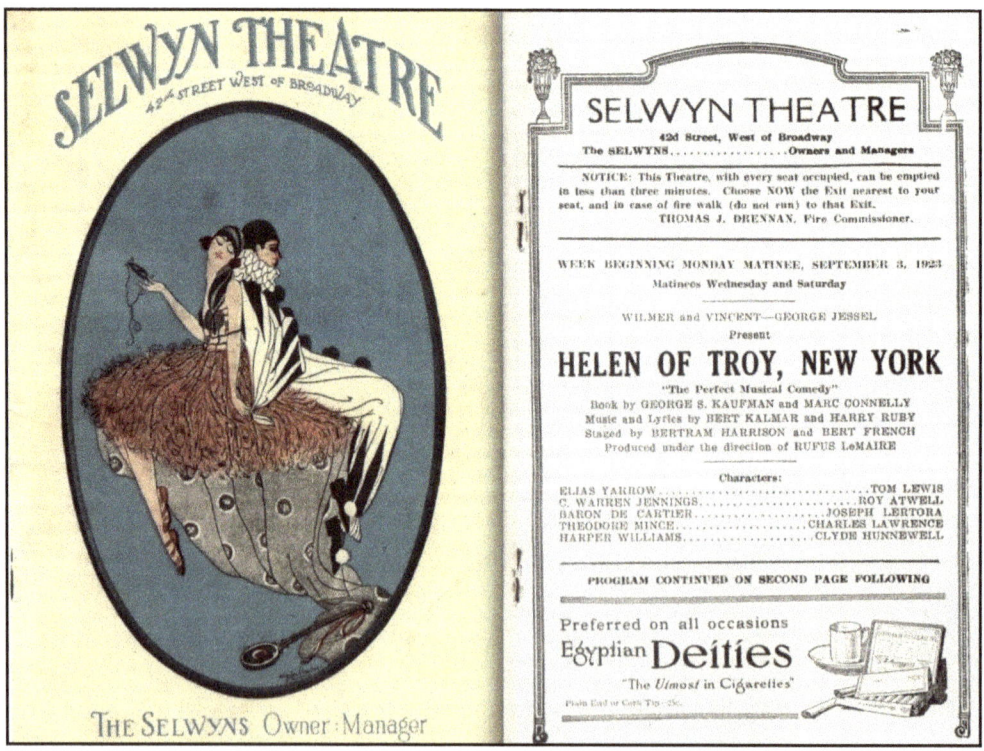

The program for Helen at the Selwyn Theater in 1923. Image from Net.

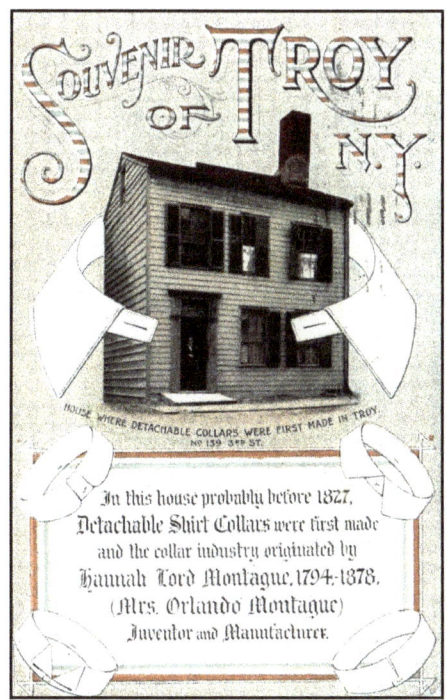

It all started in 1827 when Hannah Montaque cut off her husband's collar, washed it, and sewed it back on. A million dollar industry was born. Yes the house was torn down.

Our first choice was Troy Music Hall and the good folks at the Music Hall were agreeable to let us perform there but after realizing that we would have to do the play in July – there is no air conditioning in the Hall – and it was our first play with no track record ($$) we were forced to look elsewhere. Luckily we found Fellowship Hall attached to the Christ Church United Methodist on State Street. Talk about irony. The towering stone spire on the church is a memorial built by J. W. A. and George B. Cluett, in memory of their parents, William and Ann Cluett, who were members of the church. Yes, the same Cluett folks who created Cluett and Peabody, & Co, the collar company that Kaufman is spoofing in *Helen*.

So it has taken eight decades to get *Helen* here and I hope you come and enjoy the play. I guarantee you will be humming some of the songs for a week. You can also win some cool prizes. Each night I will give a clue based on some historical aspect of the play. One lucky winner each night will receive a gift donated by either Manory's, The Beat Shop, Three Chicks, and a Pea, and a chance to get one of my Troy history books.

We have invited George Kaufman's daughter Ann, who is now in her 90s, to come to see the show.

You can purchase tickets online at Ticker River. Go to www.ticketriver.com and type in "Helen of Troy." Or you can call 518 378 9256 to use your credit card. You can also pay by check.

Dates: July 9, 10, 12, 17, 18 19.

Arrow Collars everywhere. Image from the Net.

Justyna Kostek (left) is a theater director from Europe and is codirecting the play with Don Rittner. She is also playing the role of the Baron de Cartier (right). Photos by Don Rittner.

Time: 7 PM except for July 12 and 19 which is a matinee at 2 PM.

Helen of Troy, New York
by George S. Kaufman and Marc Connelly

DIRECTORS
Don Rittner, (USA) & Justyna Kostek (Denmark/Poland)

CAST
James Hulihan (Elias Yarrow), Lonnie Honsinger (C. Warren Jennings), Joanna Brumley (Helen McGuffey), Kevin Rittner (David Williams), Olga N. Bogdanova (Grace), Justyna Kostek (Baron De Cartier), Anthony Scanu (Harper Williams), Alisa Serdyuk (Maribel), Matt Bradt (Theodore Mince), Olga N. Bogdanova (Madam Pasanova), Linda Janeczek Segreto (Secretary, Lady Dimple), Lorinda Himar Kimball (Secretary, model), Mark H. Delfs & Jill Camillo (Janitors).

MUSICAL DIRECTOR
Jim Skelton (guitar).

Orignal score of the title song, Helen of Troy, NY. Seven of the original songs are performed.

Helen first review before they hit Broadway.

Helen Broadway Review.

Dance CHOREOGRAPHY
Olga N. Bogdanova

WARDROBE (period Clothing) & Props
Aurora's Boutique, Annie Patterson's Fancy Shop, Denise Poutre, Phil Sawyer, The Junk

Store.

SET DESIGN
Don Rittner and Justyna Kostek

Stage Hands

Mark H. Delfs, Jill Camillo

Sponsors

Gramercy Communications, River Street Beat Shop, Clement Art & Frame, Famous Lunch, Price Chopper, Rodney G. Wiltshire, Jr., Anasha Cummings, Ideal Supermarket, Columbia Development Companies

Update. All six performances were sold out. There is a chance it may be brought back in 2023.

Original 1923 flyer for Helen of Troy, New York.

What To Do With Troy's City Hall?

First published on June 8, 2010 at 11:31 PM

If you have been following the musical chair city hall scenario in Troy lately you must be scratching your head. Recently the city government moved out of the pie-shaped city hall on River Street to the squeezebox former Verizon building on Sixth Avenue. There was a good chance that they would move into a restored Proctor's Theater complex but now there is talk about going back to the old city hall. For some strange reason Troy – even in its heyday – never did seem to have a good handle on keeping a city hall. Let's take a refresher course.

Before incorporation as a city, the village government met in various houses in the village (read that saloons and bars like Platt Titus' Eagle Tavern). Here they began passing important legislation like restraining dogs from running wild on the streets and procuring a good town clock for the inhabitants of the village.

When Troy was incorporated as a city in 1816, it was quite a growing and bustling community but still a few decades away from becoming the 4th wealthiest city in America and an industrial powerhouse. City meetings were held in the courthouse at first but then on May 25, 1816, a committee was formed to find places to hold common council meetings. They went back to Platt Titus' tavern then later to William Philips' Inn in the 1820s and then back to Titus. Why spoil a good thing?

EAGLE TAVERN, 1803.
(Platt Titus' Inn).

As the city grew, it was apparent that the council couldn't keep meeting in taverns and so after 1845, the city started using part of the Athenaeum building built and owned by the Troy Savings Bank on First Street (now a parking lot).

On May 7, 1869, the "City-Hall Company of the City of Troy" was created and authorized a committee to locate and purchase a site to build a new city hall. The original capital was increased so the Troy Savings Bank could contribute from their funds to provide rooms in the new building for banking. The bank was to jointly own the building with the city, a business arrangement that probably would raise eyebrows in this day and age. The idea was dropped when the trustees of the bank (now First Niagara) decided to build the ornate building they have on First and State Streets. In 1875, there was a move and petition drive to buy the Athenaeum building from the bank, but then Mayor (Boss) Edward Murphy, Jr. opposed it and recommended the purchase of the Third Street burial ground instead (now Barker Park).

The Athenaeum owned by the Troy Savings was the first City Hall. Now a parking lot.

The Common Council ignored the mayor and approved the purchase of the First Street building on April 1. Murphy didn't appreciate the April Fools joke and vetoed it two weeks later on the 15th. The Third Street Burial ground was finally selected on June 8 and the Vanderheyden heirs were paid $10,000 to give up any rights to the land, even though the original Vanderheyden donated it in the first place to the village of Troy. A month later the city hired Troy architect Marcus Cummings to design the building.

Before any construction could take place the city had to move 208 people buried in the old cemetery and it took almost a month to complete (July 12-August 1). Most of them were relocated to Oakwood Cemetery. A few of the graves between city hall and the Baptist church were left including the grave of Platt Titus who died in 1833 and had operated the Eagle Tavern, later Troy House (now senior citizen housing on First

& River) and home of the common council for about 30 years.

The unmoved graves and headstones were covered over with sod and are still there. There is a small monument between the back of St Anthony's Catholic Church and the First Baptist fence that appears to indicate that in 1937 the rest of the graves were dug up and reburied at Oakwood. The stone says the graveyard was abandoned in 1873, which may account for Murphy wanting to buy it in the first place. It also says the graveyard began in 1743, which is earlier than reported in most of Troy's published histories.

Village cemetery given by the Vanderheyden's and taken by the city for the new city hall in 1876. Notice the many headstones. Photo by Don Rittner.

The new city hall building was occupied in October 1876. It was an impressive structure, 150 feet long and 83 feet wide built of Philadelphia pressed brick. A clock was placed in the tower in August 1885 and was illuminated at night by a special automatic gas device attached to a timer.

Barker Park (old on left) and today (right). Photo by Don Rittner

Stone unearthed at City Hall in 1937 describing former cemetery. Photo by Don Rittner.

In addition, a 6000-pound fire bell was placed in the tower in 1887, cast by Troy's Jones Bell Foundry Company. Strangely there are very few photographs of the interior of the building. Many exist of the exterior and several were taken when the

Troy's real first city hall was torched a few weeks before election in 1938. Rumor was to get rid of the records that would have revealed wrongdoing.   Photo by Don Rittner

Former Troy High on Fifth Ave (now parking garage) almost used as City Hall during the 1950s but politics doomed this elegant structure. Photo by Don Rittner.

building burned, under suspicious conditions, on October 28, 1938. The site became Barker Park in 1944 and in 1965 half of it was given to St. Anthony's parish for a new church.

City Hall then moved over to the Police and Fire building on State and 6th Avenue and remained there for about 30 years until the current city hall was built.

City Fathers looked at converting the former Troy High School on Fifth Avenue into city hall during the 1950s but politics kept delaying things and a leaky roof did the structure in and was torn down in 1963. It would have made a beautiful city hall.

In the mid-1970s, then city manager John Buckley wanted a brand spanking modern-looking building and hired the firm of Cadman and Droste to do the job. RPI architecture professor Ken Warriner who worked for the firm was first-rate and one

City Hall was above the Fire House on State Street for about 30 years. Photo by Don Rittner.

hell of a nice person and designed the current city hall. Some have hated it from the beginning and some liked the bold new look at the time

What is certain is the Verizon building now being used is deplorable and not worthy of a city with the rich history it has. There are efforts to convert the old commercial part of Proctor's Theater into city hall and that makes a lot of sense. Some suggest that it is better to rehab the old one and move back. Not a bad idea either. Either way, the argument that the old city hall was at the center of town is not true. The center of Troy government has moved throughout the years beginning on First Street between River and State (the present Monument Square was actually Washington Square and was used as a staging area for troops), to Third Street, to State Street, then to River Street, and now along the former railroad tracks on Sixth Avenue. The center of town has never been the location of city hall but rather the area surrounding Market, Fulton, and Chatham Squares.

Instead of spending thousands of dollars to tear down city hall, perhaps a better use of that money would be to use it to convert it into a city museum. A city with such

It ain't pretty but it could serve as a nice city museum. Photo by Don Rittner.

rich history deserves a monument to that history. As such, the modern look of this building is quite suited for a museum. The story of the early natural history, Native Americans, village and city history, and its industrial and commercial rise can easily be told on the various floors and old council chambers. It can be connected to the cultural center to the north of the building, the Art Center further

River Street East Side from Fulton to Grand. Photo by Don Rittner.

River Street West between Fulton and Grand. Now park. Photo by Don Rittner.

north, and a park and dock can be developed behind and next to the museum. Combine this with a restored Proctor's Theater three blocks to the east it is clear to me that this would be a major attraction to bring people back to downtown Troy and the riverfront and would spur new retail and commercial establishments on the Broadway corridor between them.

I would then suggest that the park on the north side of Elbow Street (Fulton) be redeveloped back to a major commercial center as it was before the days of Urban Removal, or as the government called it Urban Renewal (what a misnomer that was). That area from Fulton to the river has been dismal as a park. There were more than 65 buildings torn down between Fulton and Grand during the wrecking period of the 60s and 70s. That included the Troy Theater, several department stores (like Denby's and Peerless), and many other vibrant businesses.

However, if none of this impresses you perhaps the city can do what it originally did – just start meeting at a tavern, such as Brown's Brewing Co., Ryan's Wake, or the Ale House. After all, it seems the council did a lot of the people's work while spending all those years at Platt Titus's Eagle Tavern. Maybe it will work again? There is something about having camaraderie over a good beer.

The area from Fulton to Grand today is a ghost town compared to the 60's when urban renewal leveled more than 60 historic buildings. Photo by Don Rittner.

"X" Didn't Always Mark The Spot

First published on July 9, 2014, at 7:34 PM

You know the old saying, "X" marks the spot. Well in the old days "O" marked the spot and so did "Arrows."

In the early days of aviation, before radar, satellite tracking, and radio communication, the pilot had to rely more on his or her skills and a little help from friends.

Getting your mail of course started with the penny postman in the early 19th century and then the Pony Express in the mid-19th century, followed by hot air balloons, stagecoaches, railroads, and eventually the airplane.

The first use of delivering mail by airplane is attributed to Fred Wiseman in 1911 when he carried three letters from Petaluma to Santa Rosa, California. The first official airmail drop was made by Sir Walter George Windham in British India in 1911 when his pilot delivered 6500 letters to Naini from Allahabad, a distance of only 8 miles.

In 1920 an official airmail route across America was established, all 2,629 miles of it. Since there was little navigation equipment the Postal Service in 1924 developed a not-so-pretty ground-based system for their airmail pilots. They built about 1500 beacons spaced about 3 to 5 miles apart. The beacons were 50 feet high with rotating lights placed on concrete foundations in the shape of large arrows that ranged from 50 to 70 feet long and were painted bright yellow. The beacons powered by acetylene gas flashed every 10 seconds similar to today's strobe lights. They could be seen for 10 miles and below them a series of red and green lights that flashed out, in Morse code, the letter to identify which beacon they were approaching.

The beacons were successful and more than 500 beacons were doing their job in the first year of operation. The beacon program continued until 1929. As they were improved, the beacons became 10 miles apart with stronger lights and were visible for 40 miles in good weather. However by the 1930s when radio technology had improved to such a degree the Low-Frequency Radio Range system began replacing the beacons. By 1933, the depression and high cost of operations put the beacons out of business. By the Second World War, many were taken down and used as scrap for the war effort. The last beacon was closed in 1973 but one article says the

Montana Dept. of Transportation Aeronautic Division still operated about 19 updated beacons in the hills of Western Montana.

What is fascinating is that many of the arrows are still around and while they lost their yellow hue and some have weeds growing in them, they can still be seen and appreciated. For a great read and wonderful photos visit

http://sometimes-interesting.com/2013/12/04/concrete-arrows-and-the-u-s-airmail-beacon-system/

You can download the Air Marker guide published by the government in 1945 here:

http://sometimesinteresting.files.wordpress.com/2013/12/1945-caa-air-marking.pdf

There were several types of air markers beside the arrows. The government publication states that there were seven:

1   The painted roof town marker
2   Painted highway marker
3   Illuminated day and night marker
4   Baked enamel or porcelain raised marker
5   Raised metal marker
6   Raised wood marker

7   Crushed stone or concrete marker

There are some pretty interesting photos of the examples in the publications.
There is a great color map of the air route here:
http://sometimesinteresting.files.wordpress.com/2013/12/air-travel-1929-original.jpg

The Aviation Heritage Museum of the Grants Milan airport in New Mexico has restored its airway beacon.
http://sometimesinteresting.files.wordpress.com/2013/12/grants-milan-beacon.jpg

Here is one of the abandoned arrows:
http://sometimesinteresting.files.wordpress.com/2013/11/airmail-beacon-8.jpg

Here is one on Google Maps

https://www.google.com/maps/place/
37%C2%B010'50.0%22N+113%C2%B024'01.4%22W/
@37.180561,-113.400407,152m/data=!3m1!1e3!4m2!3m1!1s0x0:0x0?hl=en

Interestingly there were arrow and beacon locations in the capital district probably as mail carriers flew north and south and then west.

Here are the locations at the end of the article. See if you can find any remains and let me know. We will publish them.

There was also the use of circles to denote an airport from the sky. Julie O'Connor posted one that was in the local newspaper when a circle was placed at Quentin Roosevelt Field on what is now the Port of Albany. Circles were used to denote a landing strip or airport. Albany was commended for putting its 10-foot wide circle of lime to help aviators find the airport on July 13, 1927. It also said the city was looking at installing lighting systems at the cost of $10,000 approved by the city council.

You can see several circles marking the spot of some abandoned airways at
http://www.airfields-freeman.com/PA/Airfields_PA_Philly_NE.htm

Particularly look at the Silver Star Airport, the Somerton Airport in Philadelphia, the Boulevard airport in Philadelphia, and Buehl Field in Bensalem, PA.

Lt. Quentin Roosevelt

"X" did mark the spot but The "X" was used on an airport but only to designate it as closed. See the Budd and Buehl Airfield photos on the previous Web site.

Speaking of Quentin Roosevelt Field. It was the region's first real airport and first municipal landing site in the nation. Quentin Roosevelt Field began as a small patch, a former polo field, on the old Shaker Farms property on Old Loudonville Road in Colonie. QR Field in Loudonville was 900 feet long and 750 feet wide. It lasted one year.

Flyers like Warren White, Cy Bytner, and the Cryer Brothers, Dale, and Ernie, flew in an open cockpit plane to deliver the mail from there. While flights were few and far between night men kept a log of all the mail planes that passed over the field. The mail planes bound for Buffalo and Cleveland followed the Hudson to Albany and then headed west.

QR was named after Teddy Roosevelt's son who was killed in WW I and crashed after being shot in the head on July 14, 1918, while fighting the German "Flying Circus." of which the Red Baron (Manfred von Richthofen) was part of? He was shot down and crashed at Chamery France. There is a good description of it in Eddie Rickenbacker's biography here:

http://www.richthofen.com/rickenbacker/

Here is a film showing members of the German "Flying Circus."

And another interesting one of the death of the Red Baron:

http://www.youtube.com/watch?v=GlRebi9GjUo

A description of Quentin is here:

http://ww2gravestone.com/general/roosevelt-quentin

QF in Loudonville

On June 19, 1919, five airplanes took off from QR and flew to Albany performing stunts above the city, looping the loop, doing tall spins, spiral dives, and turns for the benefit of hundreds of spectators who flocked to the center of the city to watch. The planes were on their way to Cornell to celebrate their centennial celebration and one of the members, a mechanic was a "Full Blooded Indian," exclaimed the papers, Sergeant Emil E Steininger, full blood Cherokee. Guess it was news that they had an "Indian."

On June 21, 1919, flying became a popular pastime in the Capital District as the newly formed Birch Aircraft Corporation advertised they would take 100 passengers on a ten-mile trip at $10 each at QR Field in Loudonville. It was reported that if flying became popular a new Curtis N J-4 of the G type plane would be installed in Saratoga Springs and if in demand regular service between Albany and Saratoga would be established and eventually to Lake George. The company thought they would be able to land at the Saratoga Race track grounds but was refused. They did get a field called the Marvin Flyer Field on South Broadway opposite the Lincoln

Bathhouse, which opened on June 2, 1919. On August 12, 1919, Major Sidney F. Parker of the British Air Service stopped at QR Field and let off Commodore Albert Traver of the Poughkeepsie Yacht Club who rode to Albany with him.

Sometime after QR Field moved to Albany around 1920 to a small patch on Westerlo Island, then being developed into the Port of Albany. In 1926 the Port announced a plan to expand lanes on QR Field there for mail, passenger, and freight service. The newly expanded field would even have a hook for dirigibles. It was called the Quentin Roosevelt Memorial Field.

On July 28, 1927, Charles Lindbergh with the Spirit of St Louis stopped at the Albany field during his national tour and landed at QR field at 10:01 AM. He left Albany to go to Schenectady and stopped there before his continuation to Syracuse for the night. While here his old flying instructor William Winston from Glens Falls visited him. He was greeted in Albany and taken to Lincoln Park where he addressed a school group and then had dinner at the Ten Eyck Hotel.

Also in 1927, Richard E Byrd, North Pole flyer with Floyd E. Bennett his pilot on the Polar Dash stopped at QR on Aug 6 on his way to Rome to take part in the Fort Stanwix/Oriskany Sesquicentennial celebration.

On Aug 10, 1927, the first women aviator landed at QR field on Westerlo Island. Ms. Bessie Davis landed with a passenger from Detroit. As the Albany newspaper editorial put it, "History is merely repeating itself. The first woman aviator lands in Albany. Some day there will be many of them. Many families will have planes. There need be no doubt about it."

On Feb 28, 1928, Charles Lindbergh arrived in the area again to see Gov. Smith sign the first State law on Aviation but instead of landing at Westerlo island in Albany, he landed in Schenectady due to the danger of cross winds in Albany.

On June 1, 1928 airmail service began in Albany at the QR Field and the new airport was developed at the Shaker Farm (now Albany Airport). QR Field was eventually abandoned after the new Albany Airport opened officially on October 3, 1928.

Rensselaer County
MZ1975 Renns

```
PROGRAM = datasheet95, VERSION = 8.5
1       National Geodetic Survey,   Retrieval Date = JULY  9, 2014
MZ1975 ***********************************************************************
MZ1975  DESIGNATION -  TURNER MT RED AND WHITE BN 2A
MZ1975  PID         -  MZ1975
MZ1975  STATE/COUNTY-  NY/RENSSELAER
MZ1975  COUNTRY     -  US
MZ1975  USGS QUAD   -  STEPHENTOWN CENTER (1945)
MZ1975
MZ1975                         *CURRENT SURVEY CONTROL
MZ1975  _____
MZ1975* NAD 83(1996) POSITION- 42 32 25.83695(N) 073 27 23.57760(W) ADJUSTED
MZ1975* NAVD 88 ORTHO HEIGHT -    506.   (meters)    1660.   (feet) SCALED
MZ1975  _____
MZ1975  GEOID HEIGHT    -        -30.73  (meters)                   GEOID12A
MZ1975  LAPLACE CORR    -          8.67  (seconds)                  DEFLEC12A
MZ1975  HORZ ORDER      -      THIRD
MZ1975
MZ1975.The horizontal coordinates were established by classical geodetic methods
MZ1975.and adjusted by the National Geodetic Survey in January 1999.
MZ1975.
MZ1975.The orthometric height was scaled from a topographic map.
MZ1975.
MZ1975.The Laplace correction was computed from DEFLEC12A derived deflections.
MZ1975.
MZ1975. The following values were computed from the NAD 83(1996) position.
MZ1975;
MZ1975;            North        East    Units Scale Factor Converg.
MZ1975;SPC MA M -  922,949.750  39,294.404   MT  0.99998211   -1 18 51.4
MZ1975;SPC MA M -3,028,044.30   128,918.39  sFT  0.99998211   -1 18 51.4
MZ1975;SPC NY E -  412,160.821  235,707.070  MT  0.99999035   +0 42 19.9
MZ1975;SPC NY E -1,352,230.96   773,315.61  sFT  0.99999035   +0 42 19.9
MZ1975;UTM  18  -4,710,945.609  626,738.819  MT  0.99979763   +1 02 37.3
MZ1975
MZ1975!           - Elev Factor x  Scale Factor =   Combined Factor
MZ1975!SPC MA M   -  0.99992549 x   0.99998211  =      0.99990760
MZ1975!SPC NY E   -  0.99992549 x   0.99999035  =      0.99991584
MZ1975!UTM  18    -  0.99992549 x   0.99979763  =      0.99972314
MZ1975
MZ1975                      SUPERSEDED SURVEY CONTROL
MZ1975
MZ1975  NAD 83(1996)- 42 32 25.83766(N)     073 27 23.57870(W) AD(     ) 3
MZ1975  NAD 83(1996)- 42 32 25.83781(N)     073 27 23.57875(W) AD(     ) 3
MZ1975  NAD 83(1992)- 42 32 25.83818(N)     073 27 23.57900(W) AD(     ) 3
MZ1975  NAD 83(1992)- 42 32 25.83842(N)     073 27 23.57925(W) AD(     ) 3
MZ1975  NAD 83(1986)- 42 32 25.83852(N)     073 27 23.57869(W) AD(     ) 3
MZ1975  NAD 27      - 42 32 25.55005(N)     073 27 25.18466(W) AD(     ) 3
MZ1975
MZ1975.Superseded values are not recommended for survey control.
MZ1975.
MZ1975.NGS no longer adjusts projects to the NAD 27 or NGVD 29 datums.
MZ1975.See file dsdata.txt to determine how the superseded data were derived.
MZ1975
MZ1975_U.S. NATIONAL GRID SPATIAL ADDRESS: 18TXN2673810945(NAD 83)
MZ1975
MZ1975_MARKER: 22 = AIRWAY BEACON
MZ1975
MZ1975  HISTORY     - Date     Condition       Report By
MZ1975  HISTORY     - 1938     FIRST OBSERVED  CGS
MZ1975
MZ1975                       STATION DESCRIPTION
MZ1975
MZ1975'DESCRIBED BY COAST AND GEODETIC SURVEY 1938 (APR)
MZ1975'SEE STATION TURNER

*** retrieval complete.
Elapsed Time = 00:00:02
```

There is a great Web site called Arrows Across America which has photos of many of the existing Air Mail arrows. There are currently shown 126 concrete arrows, 6 metal arrows and other types.

You can view them at https://www.dreamsmithphotos.com/arrow/

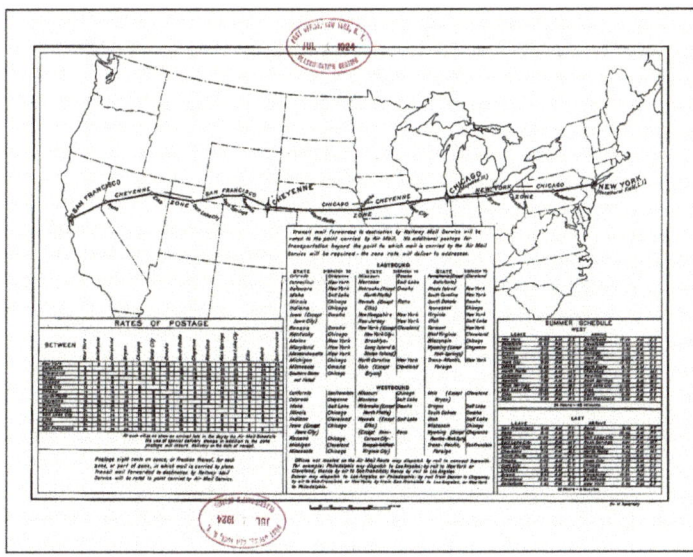

Map from 1924 created by the US Post Office Department showing the First Transcontinental Air Mail Route stretching from New York to San Francisco. The route opened on July 1, 1924, and marked the start of both day and night time air flights.

Montgomery County

NA2090 Mont

NA2085 Mont

NA2025 Mont

NA2010 Mont

```
PROGRAM = datasheet95, VERSION = 8.5
1        National Geodetic Survey,   Retrieval Date = JULY  9, 2014
 NA2090 ***********************************************************************
 NA2090  DESIGNATION -  FORT PLAIN AIRWAY BEACON 39
 NA2090  PID         -  NA2090
 NA2090  STATE/COUNTY-  NY/MONTGOMERY
 NA2090  COUNTRY     -  US
 NA2090  USGS QUAD   -  FORT PLAIN (1944)
 NA2090
 NA2090                         *CURRENT SURVEY CONTROL
 NA2090  ______________________________________________________________________
 NA2090* NAD 83(1996) POSITION- 42 58 28.49640(N) 074 41 38.39268(W)   ADJUSTED
 NA2090* NAVD 88 ORTHO HEIGHT -          **(meters)           **(feet)
 NA2090  ______________________________________________________________________
 NA2090  LAPLACE CORR    -          2.91  (seconds)                    DEFLEC12A
 NA2090  GEOID HEIGHT    -        -31.19  (meters)                     GEOID12A
 NA2090  HORZ ORDER      -  THIRD
 NA2090
 NA2090.The horizontal coordinates were established by classical geodetic methods
 NA2090.and adjusted by the National Geodetic Survey in January 1999.
 NA2090.
 NA2090.The Laplace correction was computed from DEFLEC12A derived deflections.
 NA2090
 NA2090. The following values were computed from the NAD 83(1996) position.
 NA2090
 NA2090;                    North         East     Units Scale Factor Converg.
 NA2090;SPC NY E     -   459,866.774   134,176.279   MT  0.99990308   -0 07 56.1
 NA2090;SPC NY E     - 1,508,746.24    440,210.01   sFT  0.99990308   -0 07 56.1
 NA2090;UTM  18      - 4,758,037.635   524,952.008   MT  0.99960766   +0 12 30.9
 NA2090
 NA2090                        SUPERSEDED SURVEY CONTROL
 NA2090
 NA2090  NAD 83(1986)-  42 58 28.49924(N)    074 41 38.39385(W) AD(        ) 3
 NA2090  NAD 27      -  42 58 28.24200(N)    074 41 39.87600(W) AD(        ) 3
 NA2090
 NA2090.Superseded values are not recommended for survey control.
 NA2090
 NA2090.NGS no longer adjusts projects to the NAD 27 or NGVD 29 datums.
 NA2090.See file dsdata.txt to determine how the superseded data were derived.
 NA2090
 NA2090_U.S. NATIONAL GRID SPATIAL ADDRESS: 18TWN2495258037(NAD 83)
 NA2090
 NA2090
 NA2090  HISTORY     - Date     Condition        Report By
 NA2090  HISTORY     - 1942     MONUMENTED       CGS
 NA2090
 NA2090                        STATION DESCRIPTION
 NA2090
 NA2090'DESCRIBED BY COAST AND GEODETIC SURVEY 1942 (KBJ)
 NA2090'THIS BEACON HAS FOR BASE A FOUR-LEGGED STEEL STRUCTURE ABOUT 65
 NA2090'FEET HIGH PAINTED RED AND WHITE ALTERNATELY.  IT IS LOCATED ON
 NA2090'THE FARM PROPERTY OF MR. CHARLES BRAMER.
 NA2090'
 NA2090'TO REACH THE BEACON FROM THE JUNCTION OF HIGHWAYS 5-S, 80, AND
 NA2090'163 IN FORT PLAIN, GO W ON HIGHWAY 5-S FOR 4.8 MILES TO A ROAD
 NA2090'LEADING RIGHT INTO THE FRONT YARD OF THE FARM PROPERTY OF
 NA2090'MR. CHARLES BRAMER.  TURN RIGHT AND CONTINUE AROUND BARNS AND
 NA2090'UP THE HILL FOR 0.2 MILE TO THE BEACON.

*** retrieval complete.
Elapsed Time = 00:00:02
```


```
PROGRAM = datasheet95, VERSION = 8.5
1        National Geodetic Survey,   Retrieval Date = JULY  9, 2014
 NA2090 ***********************************************************************
 NA2090  DESIGNATION -  FORT PLAIN AIRWAY BEACON 39
 NA2090  PID         -  NA2090
 NA2090  STATE/COUNTY-  NY/MONTGOMERY
 NA2090  COUNTRY     -  US
 NA2090  USGS QUAD   -  FORT PLAIN (1944)
 NA2090
 NA2090                         *CURRENT SURVEY CONTROL
 NA2090  ______________________________________________________________________
 NA2090* NAD 83(1996) POSITION- 42 58 28.49640(N) 074 41 38.39268(W)   ADJUSTED
 NA2090* NAVD 88 ORTHO HEIGHT -          **(meters)           **(feet)
 NA2090  ______________________________________________________________________
 NA2090  LAPLACE CORR    -          2.91  (seconds)                    DEFLEC12A
 NA2090  GEOID HEIGHT    -        -31.19  (meters)                     GEOID12A
 NA2090  HORZ ORDER      -  THIRD
 NA2090
 NA2090.The horizontal coordinates were established by classical geodetic methods
 NA2090.and adjusted by the National Geodetic Survey in January 1999.
 NA2090.
 NA2090.The Laplace correction was computed from DEFLEC12A derived deflections.
 NA2090
 NA2090. The following values were computed from the NAD 83(1996) position.
 NA2090
 NA2090;                    North         East     Units Scale Factor Converg.
 NA2090;SPC NY E     -   459,866.774   134,176.279   MT  0.99990308   -0 07 56.1
 NA2090;SPC NY E     - 1,508,746.24    440,210.01   sFT  0.99990308   -0 07 56.1
 NA2090;UTM  18      - 4,758,037.635   524,952.008   MT  0.99960766   +0 12 30.9
 NA2090
 NA2090                        SUPERSEDED SURVEY CONTROL
 NA2090
 NA2090  NAD 83(1986)-  42 58 28.49924(N)    074 41 38.39385(W) AD(        ) 3
 NA2090  NAD 27      -  42 58 28.24200(N)    074 41 39.87600(W) AD(        ) 3
 NA2090
 NA2090.Superseded values are not recommended for survey control.
 NA2090
 NA2090.NGS no longer adjusts projects to the NAD 27 or NGVD 29 datums.
 NA2090.See file dsdata.txt to determine how the superseded data were derived.
 NA2090
 NA2090_U.S. NATIONAL GRID SPATIAL ADDRESS: 18TWN2495258037(NAD 83)
 NA2090
 NA2090
 NA2090  HISTORY     - Date     Condition        Report By
 NA2090  HISTORY     - 1942     MONUMENTED       CGS
 NA2090
 NA2090                        STATION DESCRIPTION
 NA2090
 NA2090'DESCRIBED BY COAST AND GEODETIC SURVEY 1942 (KBJ)
 NA2090'THIS BEACON HAS FOR BASE A FOUR-LEGGED STEEL STRUCTURE ABOUT 65
 NA2090'FEET HIGH PAINTED RED AND WHITE ALTERNATELY.  IT IS LOCATED ON
 NA2090'THE FARM PROPERTY OF MR. CHARLES BRAMER.
 NA2090'
 NA2090'TO REACH THE BEACON FROM THE JUNCTION OF HIGHWAYS 5-S, 80, AND
 NA2090'163 IN FORT PLAIN, GO W ON HIGHWAY 5-S FOR 4.8 MILES TO A ROAD
 NA2090'LEADING RIGHT INTO THE FRONT YARD OF THE FARM PROPERTY OF
 NA2090'MR. CHARLES BRAMER.  TURN RIGHT AND CONTINUE AROUND BARNS AND
 NA2090'UP THE HILL FOR 0.2 MILE TO THE BEACON.

*** retrieval complete.
Elapsed Time = 00:00:02
```


```
-----------------------------------------------------------------------------
-   This listing contains control for which complete digital               -
-   data sheets where not provided.  The complete data sheets were         -
-   not provided for the reason listed below.  The reason below is         -
-   associated with a horizontal control Nonpub code shown under           -
-   the heading 'H' and/or a vertical control Nonpub code shown under      -
-   the heading 'v'                                                        -
-                                                                          -
-   The format of the records are as follows:                              -
-        Pid  = Station Permanent Identifier)                              -
-        Name = Station Designation                                        -
-        Lat  = Approx. Latitude (Degrees, Minutes, truncated Seconds)     -
-        Lon  = Approx. Longitude (Degrees, Minutes, truncated Seconds)    -
-        O    = Horizontal Order                                           -
-        o    = Vertical Order                                             -
-        H    = Horizontal Nonpub Code                                     -
-        v    = Vertical Nonpub Code                                       -
-                                                                          -
-        H Nonpub HORIZONTAL CONTROL NONPUB REASON                         -
-        -------- ------------------------------                           -
-        B        Station is a RBN antenna                                 -
-        C        Not a publishable datum within the state                 -
-        D        No descriptive text available                            -
-        I        No NAD83 coordinates available, only IGS08 coordinates   -
-        L        CORS L1 Phase Center is not publishable                  -
-        N        No geodetic control                                      -
-        O        Outside NGS publication area                             -
-        P        Purpose of position is not for network control           -
-        R        Restricted position                                      -
-        T        Station is a temporary point/bench mark                  -
-        V        Station is a VOR antenna                                 -
-        W        Weakly determined position                               -
-        X        Surface mark reported destroyed                          -
-        Y        Surface and underground mark reported destroyed          -
                                                                           -
-        v Nonpub VERTICAL CONTROL NONPUB REASON                           -
-        -------- ------------------------------                           -
-        C        Not a publishable datum within the state                 -
-        D        No descriptive text available                            -
-        F        Bench mark not yet adjusted                              -
-        N        No geodetic control                                      -
-        L        CORS L1 Phase Center is not publishable                  -
-        O        Outside NGS publication area                             -
-        R        Restricted elevation                                     -
-        S        Mark is in a subsidence area                             -
-        T        Station is a temporary point/bench mark                  -
-        X        Surface mark reported destroyed                          -
-        Y        Surface and underground mark reported destroyed          -
-        Z        Presumed destroyed                                       -
-                                                                          -
-                                                                          -
-   NOTE - Stations found in this listing may still have a valid           -
-          datasheet produced by use of other publishable values.          -
-          For example, an ADJUSTED height may be non-publishable          -
-          but a good GPS height might be found on the datasheet.          -
-          This listing does not imply that values found on the datasheet  -
-          are restricted.  If it's on the datasheet, use it.              -
-                                                                          -
-----------------------------------------------------------------------------
 Pid    Name                          Lat        Lon         Elev     O o Hv
 ------ ----------------------------- ---------- ----------- -------- - - --
>NA2085 CANAJOHARIE AIRWAY BEACON 40B 42 56 45.2/074 33 24.3          3   XX
>NA2085 CANAJOHARIE AIRWAY BEACON 40B 42 56 45.2/074 33 24.3          3   NN
```


```
-----------------------------------------------------------------------------
-   This listing contains control for which complete digital               -
-   data sheets where not provided.  The complete data sheets were         -
-   not provided for the reason listed below.  The reason below is         -
-   associated with a horizontal control Nonpub code shown under           -
-   the heading 'H' and/or a vertical control Nonpub code shown under      -
-   the heading 'v'                                                        -
-                                                                          -
-   The format of the records are as follows:                              -
-        Pid  = Station Permanent Identifier)                              -
-        Name = Station Designation                                        -
-        Lat  = Approx. Latitude (Degrees, Minutes, truncated Seconds)     -
-        Lon  = Approx. Longitude (Degrees, Minutes, truncated Seconds)    -
-        O    = Horizontal Order                                           -
-        o    = Vertical Order                                             -
-        H    = Horizontal Nonpub Code                                     -
-        v    = Vertical Nonpub Code                                       -
-                                                                          -
-        H Nonpub HORIZONTAL CONTROL NONPUB REASON                         -
-        -------- ------------------------------                           -
-        B        Station is a RBN antenna                                 -
-        C        Not a publishable datum within the state                 -
-        D        No descriptive text available                            -
-        I        No NAD83 coordinates available, only IGS08 coordinates   -
-        L        CORS L1 Phase Center is not publishable                  -
-        N        No geodetic control                                      -
-        O        Outside NGS publication area                             -
-        P        Purpose of position is not for network control           -
-        R        Restricted position                                      -
-        T        Station is a temporary point/bench mark                  -
-        V        Station is a VOR antenna                                 -
-        W        Weakly determined position                               -
-        X        Surface mark reported destroyed                          -
-        Y        Surface and underground mark reported destroyed          -
                                                                           -
-        v Nonpub VERTICAL CONTROL NONPUB REASON                           -
-        -------- ------------------------------                           -
-        C        Not a publishable datum within the state                 -
-        D        No descriptive text available                            -
-        F        Bench mark not yet adjusted                              -
-        N        No geodetic control                                      -
-        L        CORS L1 Phase Center is not publishable                  -
-        O        Outside NGS publication area                             -
-        R        Restricted elevation                                     -
-        S        Mark is in a subsidence area                             -
-        T        Station is a temporary point/bench mark                  -
-        X        Surface mark reported destroyed                          -
-        Y        Surface and underground mark reported destroyed          -
-        Z        Presumed destroyed                                       -
-                                                                          -
-                                                                          -
-   NOTE - Stations found in this listing may still have a valid           -
-          datasheet produced by use of other publishable values.          -
-          For example, an ADJUSTED height may be non-publishable          -
-          but a good GPS height might be found on the datasheet.          -
-          This listing does not imply that values found on the datasheet  -
-          are restricted.  If it's on the datasheet, use it.              -
-                                                                          -
-----------------------------------------------------------------------------
 Pid    Name                          Lat        Lon         Elev     O o Hv
 ------ ----------------------------- ---------- ----------- -------- - - --
>NA2085 CANAJOHARIE AIRWAY BEACON 40B 42 56 45.2/074 33 24.3          3   XX
>NA2085 CANAJOHARIE AIRWAY BEACON 40B 42 56 45.2/074 33 24.3          3   NN
```

```
PROGRAM = datasheet95, VERSION = 8.5
1        National Geodetic Survey,    Retrieval Date = JULY  9, 2014
NA2025 ***********************************************************************
NA2025 DESIGNATION -  CLEVELAND ALBANY AWY BCN 41
NA2025 PID         -  NA2025
NA2025 STATE/COUNTY-  NY/MONTGOMERY
NA2025 COUNTRY     -  US
NA2025 USGS QUAD   -  TRIBES HILL (1980)
NA2025
NA2025                         *CURRENT SURVEY CONTROL
NA2025  _____
NA2025*  NAD 83(1996) POSITION- 42 55 21.45424(N) 074 18 26.34944(W)   ADJUSTED
NA2025*  NAVD 88 ORTHO HEIGHT -         **(meters)        **(feet)
NA2025
NA2025  LAPLACE CORR  -           0.66  (seconds)                      DEFLEC12A
NA2025  GEOID HEIGHT  -         -30.96  (meters)                       GEOID12A
NA2025  HORZ ORDER    -  THIRD
NA2025
NA2025.The horizontal coordinates were established by classical geodetic methods
NA2025.and adjusted by the National Geodetic Survey in January 1999.
NA2025.
NA2025.The Laplace correction was computed from DEFLEC12A derived deflections.
NA2025
NA2025. The following values were computed from the NAD 83(1996) position.
NA2025
NA2025;               North         East    Units Scale Factor Converg.
NA2025;SPC NY E  -   454,095.203  165,729.501  MT  0.99990304  +0 07 52.4
NA2025;SPC NY E  - 1,489,810.68   543,730.87  sFT  0.99990304  +0 07 52.4
NA2025;UTM  18   - 4,752,455.338  556,530.157  MT  0.99963931  +0 28 18.2
NA2025
NA2025                       SUPERSEDED SURVEY CONTROL
NA2025
NA2025  NAD 83(1986)- 42 55 21.45872(N)     074 18 26.34969(W) AD(     ) 3
NA2025  NAD 27      - 42 55 21.18830(N)     074 18 27.86430(W) AD(     ) 3
NA2025
NA2025.Superseded values are not recommended for survey control.
NA2025.NGS no longer adjusts projects to the NAD 27 or NGVD 29 datums.
NA2025.See file dsdata.txt to determine how the superseded data were derived.
NA2025
NA2025_U.S. NATIONAL GRID SPATIAL ADDRESS: 18TWN5653052455(NAD 83)
NA2025
NA2025_MARKER: 22 - AIRWAY BEACON
NA2025
NA2025  HISTORY     - Date     Condition         Report By
NA2025  HISTORY     - 1942     FIRST OBSERVED    CGS
NA2025  HISTORY     - 19980513 MARK NOT FOUND    USPSQD
NA2025
NA2025                          STATION DESCRIPTION
NA2025
NA2025'DESCRIBED BY COAST AND GEODETIC SURVEY 1942 (KBJ)
NA2025'STATION IS LOCATED IN THE S EDGE OF AURIESVILLE, ABOUT 6 MILES
NA2025'W OF AMSTERDAM.  IS IS A DEPARTMENT OF COMMERCE AIRWAY BEACON
NA2025'OF STEEL CONSTRUCTION, ABOUT 90 FEET HIGH AND PAINTED RED
NA2025'WHITE ON PROPERTY OWNED BY THE DEPARTMENT OF COMMERCE.
NA2025'
NA2025'TO REACH THE STATION FROM THE INTERSECTION OF N.Y. ROUTES 5S
NA2025'AND 288, AND THE POST OFFICE IN THE VILLAGE OF AURIESVILLE, GO
NA2025'S ON ROUTE 288 FOR 0.25 MILE TO FORK IN THE ROAD, TAKE RIGHT
NA2025'FORK AND GO 0.2 MILE TO AIRWAY BEACON ON THE RIGHT.
NA2025
NA2025                          STATION RECOVERY (1998)
NA2025
NA2025'RECOVERY NOTE BY US POWER SQUADRON 1998
NA2025'MARK NOT FOUND.

*** retrieval complete.
Elapsed Time = 00:00:01
```

```
PROGRAM = datasheet95, VERSION = 8.5
1        National Geodetic Survey,    Retrieval Date = JULY  9, 2014
NA2010 ***********************************************************************
NA2010 DESIGNATION -  CLEVELAND ALBANY AWY BCN 42
NA2010 PID         -  NA2010
NA2010 STATE/COUNTY-  NY/MONTGOMERY
NA2010 COUNTRY     -  US
NA2010 USGS QUAD   -  AMSTERDAM (1980)
NA2010
NA2010                         *CURRENT SURVEY CONTROL
NA2010  _____
NA2010*  NAD 83(1996) POSITION- 42 52 52.92202(N) 074 07 42.56424(W)   ADJUSTED
NA2010*  NAVD 88 ORTHO HEIGHT -         **(meters)        **(feet)
NA2010
NA2010  LAPLACE CORR  -          -1.71  (seconds)                      DEFLEC12A
NA2010  GEOID HEIGHT  -         -30.93  (meters)                       GEOID12A
NA2010  HORZ ORDER    -  THIRD
NA2010
NA2010.The horizontal coordinates were established by classical geodetic methods
NA2010.and adjusted by the National Geodetic Survey in January 1999.
NA2010.
NA2010.The Laplace correction was computed from DEFLEC12A derived deflections.
NA2010
NA2010. The following values were computed from the NAD 83(1996) position.
NA2010
NA2010;               North         East    Units Scale Factor Converg.
NA2010;SPC NY E  -   449,561.112  180,348.475  MT  0.99991133  +0 15 10.1
NA2010;SPC NY E  - 1,474,935.08   591,693.29  sFT  0.99991133  +0 15 10.1
NA2010;UTM  18   - 4,748,009.318  571,172.055  MT  0.99966232  +0 35 35.1
NA2010
NA2010                       SUPERSEDED SURVEY CONTROL
NA2010
NA2010  NAD 83(1986)- 42 52 52.92635(N)     074 07 42.56421(W) AD(     ) 3
NA2010  NAD 27      - 42 52 52.65291(N)     074 07 44.09544(W) AD(     ) 3
NA2010
NA2010.Superseded values are not recommended for survey control.
NA2010.NGS no longer adjusts projects to the NAD 27 or NGVD 29 datums.
NA2010.See file dsdata.txt to determine how the superseded data were derived.
NA2010
NA2010_U.S. NATIONAL GRID SPATIAL ADDRESS: 18TWN7117248009(NAD 83)
NA2010
NA2010_MARKER: 22 - AIRWAY BEACON
NA2010
NA2010  HISTORY     - Date     Condition         Report By
NA2010  HISTORY     - 1942     FIRST OBSERVED    CGS
NA2010  HISTORY     - 19980513 MARK NOT FOUND    USPSQD
NA2010
NA2010                          STATION DESCRIPTION
NA2010
NA2010'DESCRIBED BY COAST AND GEODETIC SURVEY 1942 (KBJ)
NA2010'STATION IS LOCATED ABOUT 3-1/2 MILES W OF PATTERSONVILLE, ABOUT
NA2010'6 MILES S OF AMSTERDAM.  IT IS A DEPARTMENT OF COMMERCE AIRWAY
NA2010'BEACON OF STEEL CONSTRUCTION, ABOUT 85 FEET HIGH, PAINTED RED
NA2010'AND WHITE AND FLASHES LOCATION LETTER ..- (U).
NA2010'
NA2010'TO REACH STATION FROM THE INTERSECTION OF N.Y. ROUTES 5S AND
NA2010'160 IN PATTERSONVILLE, GO W 3.45 MILES ON ROUTE 160 TO A T ROAD
NA2010'RIGHT, JUST BEFORE REACHING THE SCOTCH CHURCH, TURN RIGHT AND GO
NA2010'0.6 MILE TO A T ROAD RIGHT, TURN RIGHT AND GO 0.15 MILE TO AIRWAY
NA2010'BEACON ON THE LEFT SIDE OF THE ROAD.
NA2010
NA2010                          STATION RECOVERY (1998)
NA2010
NA2010'RECOVERY NOTE BY US POWER SQUADRON 1998
NA2010'MARK NOT FOUND.

*** retrieval complete.
Elapsed Time = 00:00:02
```

Saratoga County
OD1549 Saratoga

Washington County
OD1396 Wash

Yes, Virginia, There Really WAS A Santa Claus

First published on December 13, 2009, at 8:07 PM

I can't think of anything more devastating than being told there was no Santa Claus while growing up. To spare future trauma on small tots, here are the facts. There was a Santa Claus and his spirit of kindness is what we attempt to perpetuate each year. A fellow named Nicholas was born in Patara in the year 280 AD about 350 miles northwest of Bethlehem in Asia Minor. He died on December 6th, 342 or 343. He was born a Christian into a wealthy family but they died during an epidemic. Nicholas distributed his inherited wealth and became a priest, and later the Archbishop of Myra, now Demre, near the SW coast of what is now Turkey.

Demre is the Lycian town of Myra, the home of Saint Nicholas of Myra.

Bishop Nicholas developed a reputation for kindness and there are many examples. Perhaps one of the more popular stories has to do with three sisters who were too poor to have a dowry upon marriage as their father, a noble, could not raise the money.

When the first two daughters were ready to wed, the bishop tossed a bag of gold into the house at night before each of their weddings. When the third daughter was ready, the father, now wishing to find out who this anonymous donor was, kept a watch on the house. Apparently, the Bishop climbed up on the house and dropped the third bag of gold down the chimney, which fell into a wet stocking that was being hung to dry (now you know the origin of hanging stockings). The nobleman approached Nicholas and he begged to keep it

Saint Nicholas by Jaroslav Čermák.

quiet, but like today, secrets get out. After that, everyone who received an anonymous gift thanked the Bishop.

Nicholas became known for calming storms, saving children, and even making prison walls drop when victims of persecution prayed to him. When he died, his kindness became a legend and a cult developed.

Several centuries later, the Russian Emperor Vladimir, while visiting Constantinople, heard about Bishop Nicholas and his kindness and decided to make him the patron saint of Russia. Later the stories spread to the Laplands - to the people that use reindeer sleds (getting the picture yet?).

Remember the three bags of gold Nicholas gave the sisters? Merchants in northern Italy took to Nicholas, and statutes and pictures were made showing him holding the three bags. When merchants adopted him as their patron saint, the three bags became three gold balls, representing moneylenders, and today is the symbol (and patron saint) for pawnbrokers.

St. Nicholas became so popular that churches were built just for him. During the 12-13th centuries, Holland had 23 churches dedicated to him alone. Amsterdam made him their patron saint, but he also became the patron saint of judges, murderers, thieves, paupers, scholars, sailors, bakers, travelers, maidens, and poor children. There are more than 400 St. Nick churches in Great Britain and, besides being the National Saint of Russia, he holds that title in Greece too.

It is reported that in Myra, the bones of Saint Nicholas each year sweated out a clear watery liquid, called Manna and possessed immense powers. As the bones were stolen and brought to Bari, Italy, on May 9th, 1087, they continued to sweat. Even today a flask of Manna is extracted from the tomb of Saint Nicholas every year on December 6th (the Saint's feast day). A festival called the Festival of the Translation of the Relics is held in Bari each year to celebrate the bones being brought there.

So how did St. Nicholas become Santa Claus? Thank the Dutch for that one. They brought over the tradition with the establishment of New Netherland in the Northeast during the 17th century. "Sint Nikolaas," the Dutch way of saying Saint Nicholas, was corrupted to "Sinterklaas." Pretty easy to see how Sinterklaas became Santa Claus, isn't it?

The first record of the word Sinterklaas was in March 1676 in Albany when Maria Van Rensselaer went shopping at her local Albany baker. In Wouter de backer's account book, it lists all of her orders including "St Nicolas goods" (implying goodies for the kids) and she spent 2:10 Florens for it.

Today 1.75 florins equals one US dollar.

Jaap A. Jacobs, a Dutch historian from the Netherlands reminded me also that the first mention of Christmas Eve (Jaap writes that In Dutch, it is "Nicolaes avont") was on April 18, 1648, and published in Arnold J. F. van Laer (trans. and ed.), *Council Minutes, 1638-1649*. New York Historical Manuscripts: Dutch. Vol. 4. Baltimore: Genealogical Publishing Co., Inc., 1974, p. 510-511:

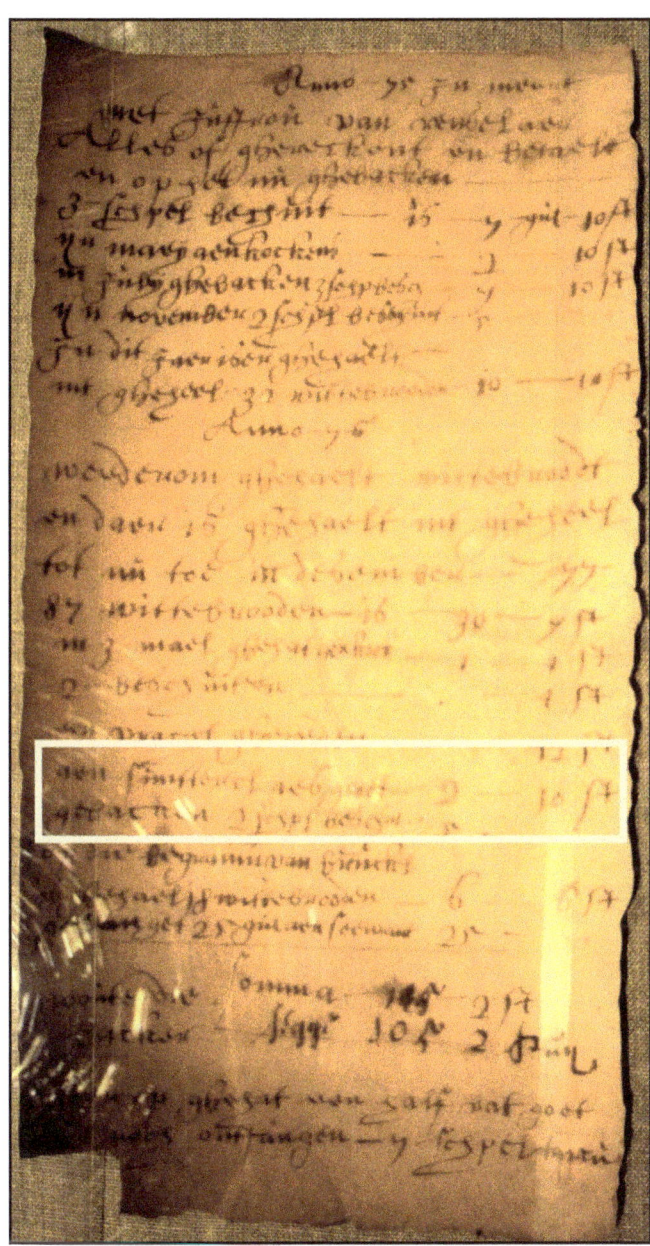

Maria Van Rensselaer's order for Christmas goodies (aen suntterclaesgoet) from her baker Wouter de backer in March 1676. This is the first record of Christmas in New Netherland. Source NYS Museum.

"Whereas Jems Hallett, at present, a prisoner, has heretofore made bold to run away from the Company's service without leave or permission and at Greenwich, within the jurisdiction of New Netherland, to steal divers goods; and furthermore has stolen a canoe from the Indians hereabout and therein, on St. Nicholas Eve, carried off a servant girl from her master's house, for which misdeed and offense he, Jems Hallett, on the third of last March, was condemned by the honorable general and council to be brought to the place where justice is usually executed, there to witness the punishment which was then and there inflicted and, in order to make satisfaction for the stolen goods, etc. to saw during an entire year, on the condition that he should receive reasonable wages for said labor if he conducted himself well."

The Feast of Sinterklaas has been an annual event in Dutch and Flemish societies for centuries. St. Nicolas Feast Day celebrated on December 6th (or Dec. 5th the eve) has been observed in most Roman Catholic countries and the Low Countries (like the Netherlands) without religious overtones. St. Nick has always been portrayed in his bishop clothes (hooded robe, red mantle and mitre (hat), a golden staff (crosier), and sporting a long white beard – and skinny, not fat).

Ironically, the town of Antalya's Archaeological Museum contains several bone fragments of the former Bishop of Myra in a 'red-lined' case. Only these few fragments have been preserved in Turkey. The rest were removed to Italy.

All Dutch kids know that Sinterklaas lives in Spain though no one knows why. It might be a connection with being the patron saint of sailors or the fact that Spain controlled much of the Dutch region for years. However, while in Spain, St. Nick keeps track of your behavior in a big red book and his assistant Black Peter gathers up enough presents to bring around on December 5th, the eve of St. Nick's day. During this time Sinterklaas jumps on his white steed Peter (not a sleigh mind you) with a huge sack of presents slung over his shoulder.

The bottom line is Santa Claus represents a time to be kind and it is in this spirit that perhaps we all show our better side – even if only once a year!

This column was originally written on December 14, 2004, but was updated.

On the left is an Ad card from Troy's Frear's Department Store during the 19th century but on the right is cartoonist Thomas Nast's drawing of Santa in 1881 which formed our modern image of what Santa looks like. It appeared in the January 1, 1881 issue of Harper's Weekly.

Missed Opportunities

First published on December 16, 2010 at 1:14 AM

The job of a preservationist is one where you try to stand firm and stop a tsunami. No matter how strong you are it's usually a losing effort. Once in a while, a landmark will stay firm and not get swept away, but those victories are few and far between, though sweet when they happen.

Historic Albany Foundation, Albany's leading preservation organization announced its endangered buildings list this past week (http://blog.timesunion.com/realestate/albanys-most-endangered-buildings/5603/). They do this every five years and call attention to the state of preservation in the city. It not only gets a chance to bring to light landmarks that are in danger but also an opportunity to show what has been saved. All too often, however, we lose more than we save.

Over the last few years, we have lost many landmarks in the Capital District and I often lament how we are missing opportunities to do the right thing by bringing them back and reaping the benefits of heritage tourism dollars, which many of them would attract. Here are a few examples.

Albany Rolling Mill and Rensselaer Rolling Mill

This is what I wrote about these two mills in 2003. Both sites are now gone.

"Two of Troy's most endangered buildings are both nationally significant - the Albany Iron Works and the Rensselaer Iron Works.

You may remember the fiasco a few months back when the U.S. Navy was recovering the turret of the Civil War ironclad U.S.S. Monitor. While they were bringing up the turret, the city had approved the semi-demolition of the Albany Iron Works, which made the hull plates. Most people know the aging old foundry building in South Troy, near the Menands Bridge, as the old Portec place. Making railroad joints was the last product that came off the assembly, until it closed in 1989, marking more than 150 years in operation. Most Civil War buffs around the country know it is one of the most important historic sites in the nation for making the iron skins for the ironclad that turned the war in favor of the North.

Five years ago, Dan Wolfe and his Troy Transfer Company obtained a 20-year lease on the property from Portec. Dan and his 25 employees use the property as a waste transfer station. Contractors bring demolition debris to the site, pay a fee, and Troy Transfer takes it to the landfill. Unfortunately, since the foundry and surrounding buildings were in disrepair, Dan began to dismantle some of the foundry. Today, a good portion of the foundry is gone - the sides and interior - and some adjacent buildings. The main foundry is still there but its ultimate fate is still unknown. Of course, if the city had any visionaries it would have purchased the site from Portec, promote my idea of rebuilding the Monitor as a tourist attraction to the Feds, and park it right next to the new Troy museum. That's right, the mill could have been rehabbed into a large Civil War museum along with the Rensselaer Iron Works and the current Burden Iron Museum. It could have attracted thousands and put millions of dollars in heritage tourism dollars in the city's coffers.

The Rensselaer Iron Works is located a few yards south of the Poestenkill and is owned by the city. Unless the city does something soon, it will probably collapse from neglect. Part of the eastern roof has already fallen in. The last real use of the mill was by Ludlow Valve, one of the area's largest valve makers. There were two buildings originally as part of this complex but the actual rolling mill burned in 1969. The Mill made rivets for the Monitor construction.

The Rensselaer Iron Works eventually became one of the largest in America. Owned by John A. Griswold, Erastus Corning Jr., and Chester Griswold, it consolidated with the Albany Iron Works in 1868, owned by Corning and company. The same year, the Bessemer Steel Works, not far from the mill, also became part of the Rensselaer Iron Works. It was owned by John Winslow, Griswold, and Alexander Holley. Holley is recognized as the Father of modern American steel manufacture. The new firm was incorporated in 1875 as the Albany & Rensselaer Iron & Steel Company and was a mammoth complex. In 1885, the company was reorganized as the Troy Iron & Steel Company. John Griswold was Mayor of Troy in 1850, raised many troops for the war, and in 1862 was elected to the House of Representatives. He also served as a trustee of RPI. He was the nephew of General Wool, the commander of Fort Monroe during the famous Monitor/Merrimac combat. In 1897, Ludlow purchased the mills on the Poestenkill and used them until they went out of business. It was owned recently by Scolite, but in a deal with the city, sold it. It's currently being rented by a firm that cuts cordwood for fireplaces, etc.

Unfortunately, those in local government see these buildings as eyesores and not the potential revenue-generating resources they can become. If you have read this column in the past, I have given numerous examples of communities around the country that are raking in millions of heritage tourism dollars by saving and promoting their local history. It is beyond reason and logic that this city does not have a director of heritage tourism. There are few cities in the entire country that has the number of historic resources Troy has - and that's after a 30-year demolition derby, which has already removed so much. Citizens should insist, no mandate, that before the next election ALL candidates for office must visit half a dozen cities in the east that have successfully promoted their local history and then come back and tell YOU what they will do to preserve Troy's great history. We deserve no less."

The following year in my Visions of Troy columns in the Troy Record I wrote:

"The Hudson River Sloop Company.
Location: Rensselaer Rolling Mill, foot of Monroe Street.
The Rensselaer Rolling Mill, (aka Ludlow Valve Company), was an important 19th-century ironworks. Among other things, it provided rivets and bolts for the USS Monitor in 1862. The city has owned the site for several years letting it deteriorate to the point that part of the roof is collapsing. Within the building are two cupola furnaces, a steam engine works, bellows, and other 19th-century industrial remains.

This building is ideal for a new shipbuilding facility where Hudson River Sloops and Schooners, as well as bateau, canoes, Dutch sailing vessels, and paper boats can be built and sold.

Once, several boat makers lined the rivers from Waterford to Albany, and hundreds of boats could be seen plying up and down the river daily. Look at any 19th-century painting of Troy or Albany! The rolling mill could be used to bring back the paper boat industry created by Eliza Waters and son George in 1867. One year after the first Waters paper boat was constructed, paper-racing hulls won 14 water races, followed by 26 wins the following year, making quite a splash with the rowing public. Visit the Burden Museum to see one of only three in existence.

Local Trojan Greg Pattison, with his BOCES students, has built replicas of the bateau, and there is an association of ice racers south of us that could perhaps bring winter sports to the area. Ice racing and sleighing were common on the river during the 19th century.

If Senator Joe Bruno's harbor plan doesn't materialize, a harbor can be created next to the sloop company so that a replica of the USS Monitor can dock there, as well as have landings for the sloop Woody Guthrie, and the 100-year-old Dutch barge, the Golden Re'al, operated by the New Netherland Co.

This project would not only create boats and jobs but would liven up the river travel between Waterford and Albany.

In a recent federal report, Civil War sites in America reported a visitation of 11,220,084. Attendance by visitors to visitor centers was 5,833,232. These parks collectively have 163 full-time positions and 129 part-time positions. In addition, 8,338 volunteers also provide visitor services in the parks. A large park-like Gettysburg reported 18 full-time permanent interpretive positions. A USS Monitor Civil War Museum Park will add to this."

Both of these buildings burned over the last few years. Only the facade of the Albany rolling mill remains.

Burden Horseshoe Complex

This is what I wrote in 2004 in my Visions column:

"Horseshoe Commons
Location: South of the Burden Museum.
This complex of five buildings is what remains of a much larger complex, the Burden Lower Works. Here horseshoes were made, stored, and shipped around the world. These buildings are unique architecturally by having truss roofs, but the buildings are falling down. Of course, the city owns them.

This complex should be renovated into a Quincy Market-style complex with a miniature golf course on the north end. A rail, which runs along the length of the longest building, can be used by the proposed trolley system and can make daily runs from here to the train station to Congress Street."

This complex, owned by the city, has been allowed to rot and several of the buildings have collapsed.

I could go on and on. The Stanford Mansion (https://web.archive.org/web/20180612205535/https://blog.timesunion.com/rittner/the-stanfords/) in Niskayuna has been stripped and moved off its original location to make way for a commercial strip mall known as – "Mansion Square." Can you believe it?

In Schenectady City, the complex of buildings that made up American Locomotive Company (ALCO) is being torn down, and not one saved for a railroad museum in the city that began railroading in New York State but many historians say was the center of railroading in the country in the earliest days (https://web.archive.org/web/20160304060810/http://blog.timesunion.com/rittner/schenectady%E2%80%99s-contributions-to-the-history-of-automobiles/426/).

All of these examples, were they located elsewhere in the country, would probably have been recognized for their historical importance to American history and saved and restored. There are so many examples of this in other communities that understand the importance of heritage tourism. In the Capital District, it seems one cannot see the forest through the trees.

Cohoes Falls An Ancient Wonder Of The New World – Again!!

First published on May 26, 2009, at 10:04 PM

As a kid growing up in Troy, it was always a treat to try and get over to Cohoes to see the great falls. The roar of the falls in the springtime and the mist that you could see from Oakwood Cemetery in Troy were proof positive that Mother Nature was making a statement here.

These ancient falls of slate and sandstone that dips eastward are now 2000 feet back from where they started, slowing eroding its bedrock over the last countless thousands of years. Cohoes has been described as an Iroquois word meaning either overturned canoe or a canoe falling. However, it most likely meant rapids or falling water as the word can be seen several times on early 17th century maps in areas that appear as rapids.

Cohoes Falls. Photo by Don Rittner

The overturned canoe theory is the result of writings by Adriaen Van der Donk, the area's first sheriff, first lawyer, first DA, first naturalist, first promoter of democracy, and author of the first book on New Netherland in 1655:

"In the area of the great falls of the Macques Kill (Mohawk River) which the Indians name the Cahoos Falls…An occurrence of this kind took place here in our time. An Indian whom I have known accompanied by his wife and child with sixty beaver skins descended the river in his canoe in the spring when the water runs rapid and the current is strongest… This Indian carelessly approached too near the Falls before he discovered the danger, and notwithstanding his utmost exertions to gain the land, his frail bark with all on board was swept over by the rapid current and down the Falls; his wife and child were killed, his bark shattered to pieces, his cargo of furs damaged. But his life was preserved."

During the 17th and 18th centuries, Cohoes Falls was revered for its beauty and power, however during the 19th century that force of power became the owner of mill owners and is today controlled by a utility company. For the last, so many years the faucet was turned off, water diverted, and only a trickle was seen falling down its 75-foot walls. As the Web site "Waterfalls of the Northeastern United States" (http://www.northeastwaterfalls.com) sadly puts it:

The Falls at Cohoes by Thomas Chambers (1808-1869)

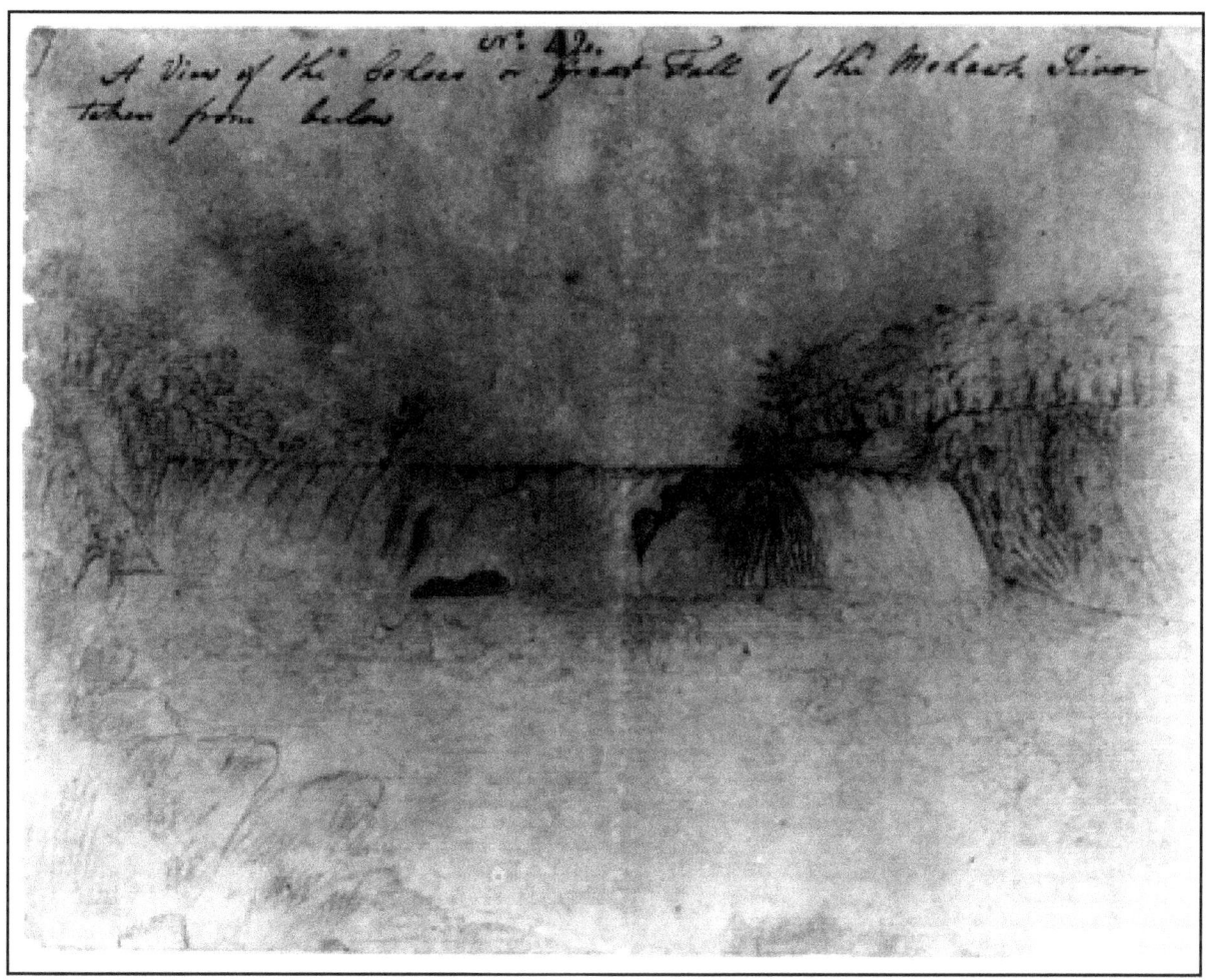

Perhaps the earliest sketch of the falls by British army officer and painter Thomas Davies (1737-1812) in 1760 and titled A View of the Cohoes or Great Fall of the Mohawk River Taken from Below.

Cohoes Falls is an enormously wide block waterfall on the Mohawk River in Cohoes. Finding a decent vantage point was moderately confusing. Eventually, a good view was found from a small park on the south side of the river. The falls would be magnificent in full spate, but we saw a wide waterfall with a lot of industrial intrusions.

Descriptions of the Cohoes Falls have been part of diaries from around the world for the last 400 years.

In 1642, the Reverend Johannes Megapolensis, the dominie in Albany, wrote to his friends:

"Through this land runs an excellent river…When we saw not only the river falling with such a noise that we could hardly hear one another, but the water boiling and dashing with such force in still

weather, that it was all the time as if it were raining…I saw there in clear sunshine when there was not a cloud in the sky… in a great abyss the half of a rainbow…of the same color with rainbow in the sky."

In April of 1660, Jasper Dankers and Peter Sluyter, two Dutch missionaries wrote:

…*"We rode to visit the Cahoos, which is the falls of the great Macquas Kill (Mohawk River) which are the greatest falls not only in new Netherlands, but in North America, and perhaps…in the whole world.*

As you come near the Falls, you can hear the roaring which makes everything tremble, but on reaching them and looking at them, you see something wonderful, a great manifestation of God's power and sovereignty of his wisdom and glory."

According to the Military Journals of Two private soldiers, 1758-1775, General Schuyler was casting up entrenchments at Cohoes Falls a few weeks before the Saratoga battles in 1777. Even General George Washington made at least one visit to the falls in 1783 during a tour of the Northern frontier.

John Maude who made a second visit to the falls and then later to Niagara in 1800 stated that he was *"more pleased with it now that I had seen Niagara than I was five years ago when I beheld it with disappointment. I then expected a grand and romantic Fall; I now amused myself by comparing its features and character with those of the many Falls which I had lately seen. Niagara overhangs its base; this [Cohoes] projects in massy abutments; the rock is of very hard quality, yet in the bed of the river, which is solid rock, the water has worn deep furrows and channels"*

The 1833 Travelers Guide through the Middle and Northern States comments that: *"The striking contrast of the torrent with the solitude of the scenery above, contribute to render the whole and unusual scene of sublimity and grandeur."*

It has been written that Hiawatha the skilled orator of the Iroquois persuaded the Seneca, Cayugas, Onondagas, Oneidas, and Mohawks to accept The Great Peacemaker's vision and band together to become the Five Nations of the Iroquois confederacy. Later, the Tuscarora nation joined the Confederacy and they became the Six Nations. Hiawatha got this vision while at the falls. Most likely the vision was the realization that Europeans were likely to push his people out, a thought sadly that became reality.

A view of the falls in 1849.

The Cohoes Falls also has been good for science. In September 1836 while workmen were digging there for Mill 3, a 5-ton Mastodon was found that stood 9 feet tall with tusks 4 ½ feet long. You can see it at the State Museum but originally it was displayed at the mills and in Troy's Harmony Hall. It lived 11,500 years ago.

The Falls has inspired many a poet such as famed Irishman Thomas Moore's 1804 "Written at the Cohos, or Falls of the Mohawk River" or Quaker turned Episcopal Minister Charles West Thomson's 1828 "On Visiting Cohoes Falls." Even recently a poem about the falls was written by Len Roberts and published by SUNY press in 1984.

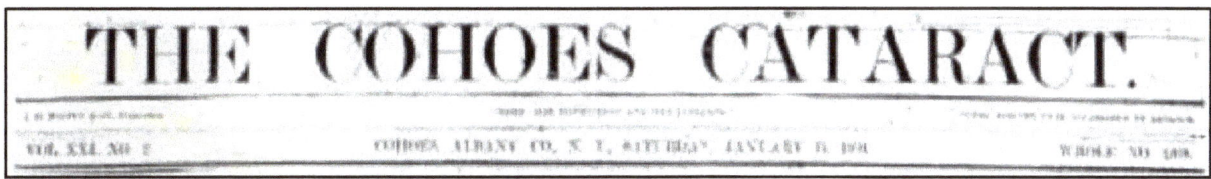

The Falls even inspired a city newspaper called the Cohoes Cataract that was published between 1849-1881.

VIEW AT COHOES FALLS.

From John Benson Lossing's The Hudson, from the wilderness to the sea / by Benson J. Lossing ; illustrated by three hundred and six engravings on wood, from drawings by the author, and a frontispiece on steel. – Published in 1866.

> **"WRITTEN AT THE COHOS, OR FALLS OF THE MOHAWK RIVER."***
>
> From rise of morn till set of sun
> I have seen the mighty Mohawk run,
> And as I marked the woods of pine
> Along his mirror darkly shine,
> Like tall and gloomy forms that pass
> Before the wizard's midnight glass:
> And as I viewed the hurrying pace
> With which he ran his turbid race,
> Rushing, alike untir'd and wild,
> Through shades that frowned and flowers that smiled.
> Flying by every green recess
> That woo'd him to its calm caress,
> Yet, sometimes turning with the wind,
> As if to leave one look behind!
> Oh! I have thought, and thinking sigh'd —
> How like to thee, thou restless tide!
> May be the lot, the life of him,
> Who roams along thy water's brim!
> Through what alternate shades of woe,
> And flowers of joy my path may go!
>
> * "There is a dreary and savage character in the country immediately above these Falls, which is more in harmony with the wildness of such a scene, than the cultivated lands in the neighborhood of Niagara. * * * The fine rainbow which is continually forming and dissolving as the spray rises with the light of the sun, is perhaps the most interesting beauty which these wonderful cataracts exhibit."

Thomas Moore's Poem of 1804.

For the last 30 years or so the falls were but a footnote in Cohoes as the city became stagnant (like Troy, Schenectady, and Albany during the same period) and virtually ignored by most. Even younger Cohosiers didn't even know there was a falls in the city! Residents of the former Mill tenements had a front row seat – sort of – the view obscured by transmission lines and wire fence. I remember bringing a friend from Virginia to visit in the 1990s and her remark was how could you take something with such beauty and turn it into such a beast?

A 1907 Photograph of the Falls.

A few years ago ownership of the falls was up for grabs as the license to generate power was up for renewal but On February 15, 2007, the Federal Energy Regulatory Commission granted Brookfield Renewable Power Inc. subsidiary, Erie Boulevard Hydropower L.P., a new 40-year license to continue operating its 38.8-megawatt School Street hydropower station on the Mohawk River.

However, as part of the deal, the Mohawk is allowed to flow over the falls year-round. They have gone further and built a brand new park on the southern end of the falls and within a week or two of this writing, you will be able to walk down and stand perhaps 10 feet from the falls themselves. Go visit and take photographs. You now have an unobstructed view!

Once again Cohoes Falls is one of the ancient — and modern —wonders of North America.

Cohoes Falls.

The Falls from Picturesque America published in 1872.

The Cataract House opened in 1860 and was a favorite hotel below the falls. Below part of the hotel can be seen.

ON VISITING COHOES FALLS.
August 1827.

I stood upon the rushing Mohawk's shore,
    And saw the waters fret and foam below,
Dashing among the rocks with angry roar,
    Like famished lions, howling when they grow

Impatient for their prey;—'tis hard to know
    The nature of our feelings—but there spread
A thrill of ecstacy, a kind of throe,
    Around my bosom, as those waters sped
With eager haste to reach their deep, unquiet bed.

To those who're cribbed in cities it is sweet
    "To catch a breath of unadulterate air,"
The wildest beauties of the hills to greet,
    And see the blooming face of nature bare—
To mark the livery which the forests wear,
    To roam the flowery fields unthralled and free,
To watch the birds, in colours rich and rare,
    Raising to heaven their song of liberty—
Such things are rapture's self—at least they are to me.

The love of nature is a part of man—
    And who would e'er forego it?—'tis a joy
To wander through her palaces, and scan
    Their grandeur and their glory—sweet employ
To trace those beauties man may not destroy,
    Her mountains and her cataracts—O yes!
I lov'd thee, Nature, from a very boy,
    And 'tis no cause that I should love thee less,
If I have known of late so seldom thy caress.

Minister Charles West Thomson's 1827 poem.

The Falls from the site of the Cataract House. Photo by Don Rittner, 2019.

Uncle Sam's Uncle Tom

First published on December 9, 2010, at 12:07 PM

The book *Uncle Tom's Cabin* has been often labeled as the kindling wood of the Civil War. Written in 1852 by Harriet Beecher Stowe, a child of a protestant preacher, it was originally penned as a set of articles for the Washington anti-slavery weekly, the *National Era*.

The mother of seven children, and a teacher, Stowe wrote to support her family. This included poetry, travel guides, biographies, children's books, and adult novels. Yet, Her name is forever etched in the annals of those who spoke against slavery during the pre-Civil War period.

Uncle Tom's Cabin piqued public interest in the subject of slavery, but it was also based on Stowe's life experiences growing up next to the slave state of Kentucky. She had firsthand knowledge about slavery, the anti-slavery movement, and the underground railroad, a network to help slaves escape to the north. In her memoirs, she gives credit to the life of the Rev. Josiah Henson whose work on the Underground Railroad inspired her writings. Henson, born in Maryland and enslaved for 41 years escaped to Canada in 1830.

The book aroused intense controversy and made Stowe a national celebrity. To help dispel the attacks on her work, she published *A Key to Uncle Tom's Cabin* the following year documenting the book's truths. She followed up with another anti-slavery novel, *Dred* in 1856. When meeting President Lincoln in 1862, he is reported to have greeted her as *"the little lady who made this big war."*

The first public performance of Uncle Tom's Cabin occurred in Troy, NY on September 27, 1852, on the stage of Peale's Museum, corner of Fulton and River. It was a family production, mostly relatives of actor George C. Howard, the museum manager. His wife Caroline, four-year-old daughter Cordelia, and George himself played major characters. George Aiken, Howard's cousin

Harriet Beecher Stowe (1811-1896). Source Wilkipedia.

Reverend Henry Highland Garnet. Source: Voice Education http://www.voiceseducation.org/category/tag/

penned the dramatic version. Another of the actors was William J. Le Moyne, who later went on to become a national stage star specializing in Dicken's works. The script ran three hours and fifteen minutes but only took the story up through little Eva's death (in fact, it has been written the play was written so it could feature Howard's daughter who played Eva). In November, Aiken rewrote and ended it with Stowe's finale. The two scripts were combined that month into a drama of six acts which became the standard acting version of the play. It was so popular in Troy, that it ran for 150 consecutive nights.

The play was performed continuously in the United States for eighty years. The Howards appeared in *Uncle Tom's Cabin* until 1857 when Howard undertook the management of the Troy Adelphi Theater, but the season failed and George, Caroline, and Cordelia went on the road eventually managing a New York theater. Cordelia retired at age 13.

Twenty years before Stowe's book was published and the play performed, the anti-slavery sentiment was in full swing in Troy. Slavery was no stranger to residents of Troy but was abolished in New York in 1827. By 1830, no slaves were living in Rensselaer County.

In November 1834, the Liberty Street Presbyterian Church at Liberty Street between

Rev. Josiah Henson 1796-1883. It was Henson's life that inspired Stowe to write Uncle Tom's Cabin. Source Uncle Tom's Cabin Historic Site (http://www.uncletomscabin.org/).

Song Sheet by George Howard. His daughter played Little Eva. Image from A Century of African American Music.

George Aiken hastily penned the dramatic version of Uncle Tom's Cabin. Image in Don Rittner's Troy: A Collar City History.

Third and Fourth gained a new paster, Rev. Henry Highland Garnet. Garnet was a leading abolitionist. His "Call to Rebellion" at the National Negro Convention in Buffalo, New York, in 1843, encouraged African Americans to resist slavery using armed rebellion. It gained him national attention.

The abolitionist movement took off in the 1830s, partly as a result of the evangelical movement that swept the north during the previous decade. It called for the end of slavery and promoted women's rights. By 1838, more than 1,350 antislavery societies existed with almost 250,000 members, including many women.

Captured runaways were taken before a Federal court or commissioner and denied a jury trial. Only the statement of the master, even if absent, was taken as the main evidence. Many people did not like this injustice and some participated in the underground railroad movement.

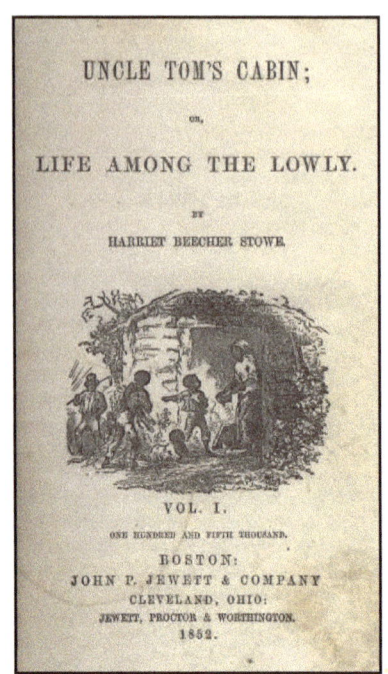

Original first edition cover of Uncle Tom's Cabin. Source: Wilkipedia.

Boardman Building on right is where Uncle Tom's Cabin was first performed in America at Peale's Museum inside. Source: Don Rittner's Troy Now and Then.

Not only was the underground railroad alive and well in Troy, but it also wasn't always underground. Our famous example is the case of Charles Nalle, a coachman for Uri Gilbert, Troy businessman, and Mayor.

On October 19th, 1848, the 28-year-old Nalle escaped from his plantation master Blucher W. Hansbrough of Culpepper County, Virginia. He worked for William Scram at Sand Lake as a teamster but told his secret to Horace F. Averill, a lawyer in Sand Lake who notified Hansbrough.

Nalle was arrested on April 27, 1860, and brought to the U.S. Commissioners' office on the second floor of a bank at the northeast corner of First and State. Several hundred people, including Harriet Tubman who was on her way to Boston, waited for Nalle to be brought out and rescued him. His freedom was purchased for $650 and returned to Troy as a free man.

You can download the original book (cut and paste this URL) at: **http://books.google.com/books?id=dLUBAAAAQAAJ&printsec=frontcover&dq=uncle+tom's+cabin&hl=en&ei=mOIATY3NBsO88ga7k9XnBw&sa=X&oi=book_result&ct=result&resnum=6&ved=0CEQQ6AEwBQ#v=onepage&q&f=false**

Entrance to Nalle's Jail cell. Photo by Don Rittner.

Inside Jail looking out. Photo by Don Rittner.

Front Door to Jail.

Peep Hole and Gun Port.

Imagine being held here with no lights in solitary confnement. Photo by Don Rittner.

Abolitionist Stoned In 1836 By Trojans

First published on April 11, 2016, at 12:21 AM

As we all know slavery was practiced in this country for many years before the Civil War. Slavery was introduced in New York in 1626 when 11 men were introduced for forced labor.

When the federal government conducted its first census in 1790, there were 1474 slaveholding families in Albany County owning 3,722 slaves. At least 23 of those families had 10-19 slaves each. Rensselaer County was part of Albany County until 1791.

By 1800, Rensselaer County had 890 slaves, decreasing to 750 in 1810, 433 in 1820, and by 1830, none. Slavery was abolished in the State in 1827.

On the reverse, 632 free slaves were living here in 1820 rising to 1058 free slaves before the Civil War began.

So from the numbers, it appears that slavery wasn't much of an issue. Not true. There were plenty of people living in the area who were pro-slavery or didn't want to get involved in the southern problem. That came real apparent one day in 1836 in Troy – the mobbing of Theodore D. Weld, a distinguished philanthropist, in Bethel, a mission church founded for the spiritual benefit of boatmen, and located on the Northwest corner of Fifth and Elbow (Fulton) streets, (for baby boomers, the site of the Fifth Avenue hotel). At that time the majority of the inhabitants of Troy were opposed to the then-increasing movement for the abolition of slavery, and many bitter controversies had arisen between the abolitionists and those who advocated noninterference with the South.

Weld had delivered several lectures on the subject of slavery and had attracted large audiences to Bethel. Soon after he had arrived in Troy there appeared in one of the city papers an incendiary letter regarding him and his teachings which stirred the proslavery people up to a high state of excitement. On the afternoon of June 2, Weld was delivering a lecture in the church before a large audience, when a mob entered and attacked him, attempting to drag him from the pulpit. A struggle between members of the congregation and the mob ensued, in which the former were victorious, after which the lecturer was conducted from the church to a place of safety by Henry Z. Hayner, a prominent lawyer who had held the leader of the mob at bay.

The incident created intense excitement throughout the city and doubtless strengthened the ranks of the local abolitionists.

The Troy Record described it better:

"While addressing the audience he was disturbed in different ways, and finally assaulted With missiles, the affair culminating in a fearful struggle which at one time was attended with great danger to all the persons assembled in the building. Amid the fray Henry Z. Hayner, Esq, a man of splendid physique and great strength, seized the ringleader of the mob at the foot of the pulpit and held him by the throat until he was black in the face. He then took Theodore D. Weld by the arm and led him through the excited, blaspheming rabble to a place of safety and escape."

Theodore Dwight Weld. From the Net.

According to one bio of Weld, he was *"born in Hampton, Conn., on November 23, 1803. He entered Phillips Andover academy in 1819 but didn't graduate based on the fact of failing eyesight. In 1830 he became general agent of the Society for the promotion of manual labor in literary institutions, publishing afterward a valuable report (New York, 1833). He entered Lane theological seminary, Cincinnati, Ohio, in 1833, but left that institution on the suppression of the Anti-slavery society of the seminary by the trustees. Weld then became well known as an anti-slavery lecturer, but in 1836 he lost his voice and was appointed by the American anti-slavery society editor of its books and pamphlets. In 1841-'3 he labored in Washington in aid of the anti-slavery members of congress, and in 1854 he established at Eagleswood, N. J., a school in which he received pupils irrespective of sex and color. In 1864 he removed to Hyde Park, near Boston, and devoted himself to teaching and lecturing. Mr. Weld is the author of many pamphlets, and of "The Power of Congress over the District of Columbia" (New York, 1837); "The Bible against Slavery" (1837); "American Slavery as it Is: Testimony of a Thousand Witnesses" (1839); and "Slavery and the Internal Slave Trade in the United States" (London, 1841). — His wife, Angelina Emily Grimké, reformer, b. in Charleston, S. C., 20 Feb., 1805, is the daughter of Judge John F. Grimké, of South Carolina, but in 1828, with her sister, (q. v.), she joined the Society of Friends in Philadelphia, afterward emancipating the slaves that she inherited from her parents in 1836. She was the author of an "Appeal to the Christian Women of the South," which was republished in England with an introduction by George Thompson, and was associated with her sister in delivering public addresses under the auspices of the American anti-slavery society, winning a reputation for eloquence. The controversy that the appearance of the sisters as public speakers caused was the beginning of the woman's rights agitation in this country. She married Mr. Weld on 14 May, 1838, and was afterward associated with him in educational and reformatory work. Besides the work noticed above, she wrote "Letters to Catherine E. Beecher," a review of the slavery question (Boston, 1837)."*

He died in Hyde Park, Mass, on February 3, 1894, relatively unknown even though some historians consider him one of the most important figures in the abolitionist movement.

For a pretty complete list of US Abolitionists and anti slavery activists go to http://www.civilwarlibrary.org/abolitionists.html

This is what the March 23, 1836 Albany Argus thought of Weld.

ANTI SLAVERY

MANUAL,

CONTAINING A COLLECTION OF

FACTS AND ARGUMENTS

ON

AMERICAN SLAVERY.

BY REV. LA ROY SUNDERLAND.

Second Edition—Improved.

NEW-YORK:
PRINTED BY S. W. BENEDICT.
1837.

Weld was not alone in anti slavery sentiments. The following year Reverend La Roy Sunderland published his Anti Slavery Manual. He was an author, orator, and manager and founding member of the American Anti-Slavery Society, December 1833, and Co-founder of Wesleyan Methodist Church.

Yes Virginia There Was Rock And Roll In The Capital District

First published on November 2, 2020, at 3:16 PM

The 20th century was the era that shaped the American music scene. Of course, there was always some form of music in this country though at first by Indigenous peoples living here, and then the importation of European music, heavily German and later French-influenced, once they arrived on the shores in the 17th century. Edward Alexander MacDowell (1861-1908) is given credit for being one of the first American orchestra composers with his "The Indian Suite," in 1892. It was based on numerous Native melodies and rhythms.

You can hear it here:
https://www.youtube.com/watch?v=vxJwLcfhK-c

As one reviewer noted, *"MacDowell was the greatest composer of classical music in the history of America."* I am well aware that it is politically correct to say that Gershwin, Copland, Ellington, and others were better, but truthfully they were not better but just different. MacDowell was writing music in a German Tradition that still dominated the musical scene throughout the 19th century. After World War I, Americans tended to be attracted to France more than to Germany, and jazz music arrived on the scene. So styles changed and the "critics" of the time name jazz music an "authentic" American genre (which it was.) Truthfully, with the history of the Twentieth Century behind us, we know now that rock played a much larger role than jazz and dominated the American scene from the 1950s to the end of the century — and that Gershwin and Ellington are products of their time just as MacDowell is a product of his. The bottom line is that we have to look at MacDowell's music based on the events and styles of his time — a time when music was dominated by Wagner and Brahms. Also, we have to look at the political correctness of referring to any composition as an "Indian" Suite when the better term is "Native American." But in MacDowell's time, they were called "Indians" and MacDowell meant his music as a beautiful tribute to "these people."

The Troy Music Hall, famous for its acoustics, was opened on April 19, 1875. Even before the city was a city, members of the Apollo Lodge, Free and Accepted Masons, purchased a bassoon, violin, and other instruments to form a band in 1797. During the early part of the 20th century, many companies like General Electric, American Locomotive, and Mohawk Carpet Mills sponsored or initiated small bands that played local gigs. Even hotels like Albany's DeWitt Clinton had its big band, Phil Romano, and his Dewitt Clinton Hotel Orchestra.

While Rock and Roll is said to have been born in the '40s and '50s, the "British Invasion" of the 60s with The Beatles, The Rolling Stones, and others completely marked a generation with songs about love and protest, and influenced daily life, fashion, attitudes, and language like nothing before it. It crossed racial barriers before that were mostly confined to regions and specific races (i.e. blues, jazz, etc.). Rock also brought in the era of heavy drug use and the resulting deaths of legends like Janis Joplin, Jimi Hendrix, and Jim Morrison brought the issue to light. Drug culture is still a big issue in music. Rock originated from musical styles such as gospel, jump blues, jazz, boogie-woogie, rhythm and blues, and country music and rock and roll got its formal name in 1954. It was performed here by the likes of Chuck Berry, Bill Halley and the Comets, and of course Elvis, but for many of us Baby Boomers, it became part of our everyday life with The Beatles and those English Bands that followed.

The Capital District was not immune to Rock and Roll. I remember going to the movies with my girlfriend Margo to see the Elvis movies. Not that I could hear it with all the girls screaming (and Margo almost pulling my hair out). My first live concert was seeing the Stones at the Palace in April 1965 (and helping remove all the furniture in their hotel rooms, but that is a different story) followed by the Dave Clark Five in Troy in July, and following years with Sonny and Cher (who I swear was singing just to me in the front row), The Doors, Jimi Hendrix and others.

The Ruins, 1966. That's me on drums. The Hideout was in Glenmont.

If you were a teenage boy (and yes even the young women wanted to get in the act), you wanted to be in a rock band and the Capital District had hundreds of them. I belonged to four rock bands, The Inertians (65), The Ruins (66), Fresh Cream (69), and Horton Strong (1970-72). There were some attempts after that but by then I was married with two kids and a full-time job. Being a rock and roll star was not meant to be although with Horton Strong we did cut demos at Vanguard and had offers by RCA. When I was playing with The Ruins a contemporary band was The Bougalieu who was able to get a single recorded (and stole our lead singer). They were one of my favorite rock bands. Of course, through the years we had popular groups like Blotto, Fear of Strangers (The Units) with lead singer Lonesome Val who I still have a crush on, The Gray Things (my cousin was their manager), Love's Ice Cubes (their bass player ended up with us), Monolith, Tino and the Revlons, the Knickerbockers, and many more. There were many places to play in the old days. Rock bands played at RPI and its fraternities (we played for most of them), Paul's on River Street in Troy, Valenti's on West Sand Lake Rd, and early on at The Escape, the basement of a church on Hoosick Street. In Albany, Bogart's, J.B. Scotts, and Refer Network's Sunday concerts in Washington Park were favorites. Other venues included The College Inn up towards Saratoga and The Hide Out in Glenmont. Many of the bars featured bands. In Troy, the famous "Strip" a row of bars on River Street from Fulton to Congress had many places and one in particular known as The Riviera had name acts (saw Sam the Sham and the Pharaohs there and The Isley Brothers in 64). Several local groups had their music recorded including The Bougalieu, Tino, The Knickerbockers, Blotto, and others like Horton Strong had their original music played on local radio stations. If you were an aspiring musician, you purchased your instruments at Hilton's (Troy & Albany), Romeo's, or George's Music Store. If you wanted to learn how to read music or take lessons, you would go over to Miller's Music Store on 4th Street in Troy. RPI's radio station, WRPI, use to have a live performance night and singers like Natalie Merchant would stop by (before she made it big). On Saturday nights,

Me on drums opening for William Kunstler at SUNYA in 1970.

you would tune in to Kaleidoscope with Jim Barrett, who still does his Kaleidoscope show and the commercial stations like WTRY and WPTR with jocks like Lee Gray and Boom Boom Brannigan would spin out the top 40 hits. Today, groups can make their own digital music, some without actual instruments, using software like Apple's Garageband. They press their CDs from their personal computer and market their homemade product on the Internet or at their gigs. You can now download music from Apple Computer into your smartphone for pennies a song and store over 1,000 songs.

In 1970, famed attorney William Kunstler then representing the Chicago 7 (the story about the trial is now on Netflix) spoke at SUNYA to 7000 people. We opened for him with the opening song "Politician" by Cream, an appropriate song for the occasion. Most of us rock and roll wannabes never made it big of course, but it sure was fun trying. In those days, getting a record contract was not easy. There was no such thing as digital music, just analog. You bought vinyl, not CDs, and having stereo meant you had two speakers. But one thing is certain. Rock and Roll is here to stay.

With Horton Strong we were the first rock band to open SPAC's 1971 season opening for The Grassroots and ended with opening for the J. Geils Band at SUNYA in October 71.

It is true that almost every legendary rock band (and other genres) played in the Albany area except the Beatles (solos by Paul and Ringo don't count) during the 20th century and to prove it below is a list of them that I compiled from various sources.

So enjoy this trip down memory lane. Many of you will have attended these concerts. I will update as needed.

ROCK AND ROLL IN THE CAPITAL DISTRICT DURING THE TWENTIETH CENTURY

Compiled by Don Rittner

1957	11/14/	The Crickets	RPI Fieldhouse	Troy
1957	11/14/	Fats Domino	RPI Fieldhouse	Troy
1960	2/21/	Dizzy Gillespie	Troy Armory	Troy
1961	11/3/	Ray Charles	RPI Fieldhouse	Troy
1962	2/23/	Dave Brubeck	RPI	Troy
1962	2/24/	Duke Ellington	RPI	Troy
1963	9/25/	Ray Charles	Palace Theater	Albany
1963	10/5/	Mantovani	RPI Fieldhouse	Troy
1963	11/4/	Benny Goodman	RPI Fieldhouse	Troy
1964	10/23/	Sonny Terry & Brownie McGhee	RPI Fieldhouse	Troy
1964	9/4/	The Beach Boys	RPI Fieldhouse	Troy
1964	2/28/	New Christy Minstrels	Troy Armory	Troy
1964	4/24/	The Brothers Four & Leon Bibb	RPI Fieldhouse	Troy
1964	10/6/	Mantovani	RPI Fieldhouse	Troy
1964	10/9/	The Kingsmen & The Chiffons	RPI Fieldhouse	Troy
1964	10/23/	Harry Belafonte	RPI Fieldhouse	Troy
1964	11/7/	Pete Seager	87 Gym	Troy
1965	4/29/	The Rolling Stones	Palace Theater	Albany
1965	2/12/	Bob Dylan	Troy Armory	Troy
1965	2/12/	Bob Dylan	Troy Armory	Troy
1965	3/5/	The Clancy Brothers & Tommy Makem	Troy Armory	Troy

Year	Date	Artist	Venue	City
1965	4/30/	Peter, Paul and Mary	RPI Fieldhouse	Troy
1965	10/15/	Isley Brothers	RPI Fieldhouse	Troy
1965	10/15/	Bobby Comstock and the Counts	RPI Fieldhouse	Troy
1965	10/16/	Dave Brubeck	RPI Fieldhouse	Troy
1965	11/12/	Jimmy Dorsey Orchestra	Troy Armory	Troy
1965	7/25/	Dave Clark Five	RPI Fieldhouse	Troy
1966	4/14/	Jerry Lee Lewis	Excelsior House	Troy
1966	3/25/	Ramsey Lewis Trio	Crooked Lake House	Averill Park
1966	3/5/	The Shirelles	Crooked Lake House	Averill Park
1966	5/6/	Ray Charles	RPI Fieldhouse	Troy
1966	5/13/	The Brothers Four	Troy Armory	Troy
1966	10/8/	Simon and Garfunkle	RPI	Troy
1966	11/11/	Peter, Paul and Mary	RPI	Troy
1967	7/24/	The Dave Clark Five	Colonie Coliseum	Latham
1967	12/8/	The Doors	RPI Fieldhouse	Troy
1967	7/24/	The Dave Clark Five	Colonie Coliseum	Latham
1967	3/3/	The Association	RPI Fieldhouse	Troy
1967	3/3/	The Rascals	RPI Fieldhouse	Troy
1967	5/5/	Sammy Davis Jr	RPI	Troy
1967	11/10/	The Lovin' Spoonful	RPI Fieldhouse	Troy
1967	12/8/	The Doors	RPI Fieldhouse	Troy
1968	4/19/	The Jim Hendrix Experience	Troy Armory	Troy
1968	2/10/	New Christy Minstrels	RPI Fieldhouse	Troy
1968	3/1/	Frankie Valli & The Four Seasons	RPI Fieldhouse	Troy
1968	4/19/	Jimi Hendrix	Troy Armory	Troy
1969	11/10/	The Who	Palace Theater	Albany
1969	10/11/	Johnny Cash	RPI Fieldhouse	Troy
1969	7/20/	The Beach Boys	Troy Armory	Troy
1969	11/14/	Sonny & Cher	RPI Fieldhouse	Troy
1969	3/8/	McKendree Spring	McNeil Room, RPI	Troy

Year	Date	Artist	Venue	City
1969	7/20/	Beach Boys	Troy Armory	Troy
1969	10/17/	Iron Butterfly	RPI Fieldhouse	Troy
1969	11/14/	Sonny & Cher	RPI Fieldhouse	Troy
1970	3/22/	The Moody Blues	SUNYA	Albany
1970	10/9/	Santana	RPI Fieldhouse	Troy
1970	2/14/	McKendree Spring	87 Gym	Troy
1970	2/24/	The Fifth Dimension	RPI Fieldhouse	Troy
1970	3/13/	Bill Cosby	RPI Fieldhouse	Troy
1970	4/11/	Van Morrison	87 Gym	Troy
1970	10/9/	Santana	RPI Fieldhouse	Troy
1971	11/16/	Jethro Tull	Palace Theater	Albany
1971	11/7/	Bill Haley & His Comets	Linda Norris Auditorium	Albany
1971	7/3/	Carl Perkins	Unknown	Albany
1971	2/11/	The Bee Gees	Palace Theater	Albany
1971	1/20/	Chicago	Palace Theater	Albany
1971	5/1/	Gordon Lightfoot	RPI Fieldhouse	Troy
1971	10/16/	Blood, Sweat & Tears	RPI Fieldhouse	Troy
1971	12/4/	The Allman Brothers	Hudson Valley Civic Center	Troy
1971	10/29/	J. Geils Band	SUNYA	Albany
1971	12/4/	J. Geils Band	Hudson Valley Community College	Troy
1971	12/4/	Allman Brothers	Hudson Valley Community College	Troy
1971	12/4/	NRBQ	Hudson Valley Community College	Troy
1972	11/29/	Eric Anderson	Palace Theater	Albany
1972	11/29/	New Riders of the Purple Sage	Palace Theater	Albany
1972	11/14/	The Beach Boys	Palace Theater	Albany
1972	3/9/	Uriah Heap	College of St Rose	Albany
1972	4/21/	Sha Na Na	Hudson River Cafe	Albany
1972	9/17/	J. Geils Band	RPI Fieldhouse	Troy
1972	9/29/	Isaac Hayes Movement	RPI Fieldhouse	Troy

Year	Date	Artist	Venue	City
1972	10/31/	Chicago	RPI Armory	Troy
1972	11/1/	Chicago	RPI Armory	Troy
1972	2/23/	Bette Midler	RPI Armory	Troy
1972	4/14/	Melanie	RPI Fieldhouse	Troy
1972	3/19/	J. Geils Band	Palace Theater	Albany
1972	3/19/	Sweathog	Palace Theater	Albany
1972	9/17/	J. Geils Band	RPI Armory	Troy
1972	8/17/	Sonny & Cher	SPAC	Saratoga
1973	11/7/	Argent	Palace Theater	Albany
1973	9/6/	New Riders of the Purple Sage	Palace Theater	Albany
1973	5/17/	Mahavishnu Orchestra	Palace Theater	Albany
1973	3/3/	The Allman Brothers	Palace Theater	Albany
1973	1/28/	Mahavishnu Orchestra	SUNYA	Albany
1973	9/28/	If & Dick Morrissey	87 Gym	Troy
1973	10/20/	The Carpenters	RPI Fieldhouse	Troy
1974	12/11/	Genesis	Palace Theater	Albany
1974	11/24/	The Kinks	Palace Theater	Albany
1974	11/10/	Jerry Garcia & Merl Saunders	Palace Theater	Albany
1974	3/8/	Seals & Croft	RPI Fieldhouse	Troy
1974	9/20/	Sha Na Na	RPI Fieldhouse	Troy
1974	10/21/	Jackson Browne	Palace Theater	Albany
1974	11/16/	America	Houston Field House, RPI	Troy
1974	11/30/	J. Geils Band	Palace Theater	Albany
1975	11/4/	Stephen Stills	Palace Theater	Albany
1975	11/2/	New Riders of the Purple Sage	Palace Theater	Albany
1975	10/14/	Black Oak Arkansas	Palace Theater	Albany
1975	10/14/	Foghat	Palace Theater	Albany
1975	10/14/	Montrose	Palace Theater	Albany
1975	9/27/	ZZ Top	Palace Theater	Albany
1975	9/5/	The Edgar Winter Group	Palace Theater	Albany

Year	Date	Artist	Venue	City
1975	8/9/	Kiss	Palace Theater	Albany
1975	4/24/	Frank Zappa	Palace Theater	Albany
1975	5/4/	New Riders of the Purple Sage	RPI Fieldhouse	Troy
1975	11/1/	Poco & McKendree Spring	Proctor's Theater	Troy
1976	12/12/	Black Oak Arkansas	Palace Theater	Albany
1976	12/12/	Montrose	Palace Theater	Albany
1976	12/12/	Rush	Palace Theater	Albany
1976	10/31/	Manfred Mann's Earth Band	Palace Theater	Albany
1976	9/20/	Blue Oyster Cult	Palace Theater	Albany
1976	9/20/	Tommy Bolin	Palace Theater	Albany
1976	9/19/	Blue Oyster Cult	Palace Theater	Albany
1976	9/19/	Tommy Bolin	Palace Theater	Albany
1976	7/2/	Utopia	Palace Theater	Albany
1976	4/22/	Styx	Palace Theater	Albany
1976	1/27/	Blue Oyster Cult	Palace Theater	Albany
1976	1/27/	Bob Seger & The Silver Bullet Bank	Palace Theater	Albany
1976	11/6/	Frank Zappa	RPI Fieldhouse	Troy
1976	10/10/	Jackson Browne and Orleans	RPI Fieldhouse	Troy
1976	11/6/	Frank Zappa	RPI Fieldhouse	Troy
1976	4/8/	J. Geils Band	Proctor's Theater	Troy
1977	12/8/	Jerry Garcia Band	Palace Theater	Albany
1977	11/17/	AC/DC	Palace Theater	Albany
1977	11/17/	Rush	Palace Theater	Albany
1977	11/3/	Dr Feelgood	Palace Theater	Albany
1977	11/3/	Gentle Giant	Palace Theater	Albany
1977	10/21/	Foreigner	SUNYA	Albany
1977	10/9/	Be Bop Deluxe	Palace Theater	Albany
1977	10/19/	City Boy	Palace Theater	Albany
1977	10/19/	Nektar	Palace Theater	Albany
1977	10/13/	Fats Domino	Turf Club	Albany
1977	1/4/	Uriah Heap	Palace Theater	Albany

1977	4/24/	Angel	Palace Theater	Albany
1977	4/24/	Max Webster	Palace Theater	Albany
1977	4/24/	Rush	Palace Theater	Albany
1977	2/24/	Dr Feelgood	Palace Theater	Albany
1977	2/24/	Gentle Giant	Palace Theater	Albany
1977	2/7/	Bruce Springsteen	Palace Theater	Albany
1977	2/2/	Boston	Palace Theater	Albany
1977	5/8/	Boston	RPI Fieldhouse	Troy
1977	7/15/	J. Geils Band	Lebanon Valley Speedway	Albany
1977	7/15/	Blue Oyster Cult	Lebanon Valley Speedway	Albany
1977	7/15/	Black Oak Arkansas	Lebanon Valley Speedway	Albany
1977	7/15/	The Dictators	Lebanon Valley Speedway	Albany
1978	5/1/	Talking Heads	Hullabaloo	Rensselaer
1978	3/4/	Talking Heads	Hullabaloo	Rensselaer
1978	12/13/	Cheap Trick	Palace Theater	Albany
1978	10/8/	Frank Zappa	Palace Theater	Albany
1978	8/23/	AC/DC	Palace Theater	Albany
1978	8/23/	Rainbow	Palace Theater	Albany
1978	7/22/	Blue Oyster Cult	Albany-Saratoga Speedway	Malta
1978	7/22/	British Lions	Albany-Saratoga Speedway	Malta
1978	7/22/	Derringer	Albany-Saratoga Speedway	Malta
1978	7/22/	Alvin Lee	Albany-Saratoga Speedway	Malta
1978	7/22/	Nantucket	Albany-Saratoga Speedway	Malta
1978	7/22/	UFO	Albany-Saratoga Speedway	Malta
1978	6/3/	REO Speedwagon	Palace Theater	Albany
1978	6/3/	Rainbow	Palace Theater	Albany
1978	5/24/	Bruce Sprinsteen	Palace Theater	Albany

Year	Date	Artist	Venue	City
1978	3/22/	Journey	Palace Theater	Albany
1978	3/22/	Van Halen	Palace Theater	Albany
1978	3/15/	Styx	Palace Theater	Albany
1978	3/5/	Be Bop Deluxe	Palace Theater	Albany
1978	3/5/	Starz	Palace Theater	Albany
1978	3/1/	Outlaws	Palace Theater	Albany
1978	3/1/	Sea Level	Palace Theater	Albany
1978	11/12/	Bruce Sprinsteen	RPI Fieldhouse	Troy
1978	5/7/	Grateful Dead	RPI Fieldhouse	Troy
1978	2/6/	Emerson, Lake & Palmer	RPI Fieldhouse	Troy
1978	5/7/	Grateful Dead	RPI Fieldhouse	Troy
1978	11/12/	Bruce Springsteen	RPI Fieldhouse	Troy
1979	12/9/	Rainbow	Palace Theater	Albany
1979	12/2/	Outlaws	Palace Theater	Albany
1979	10/12/	Commander Cody Band	JB Scott's Theater	Albany
1979	6/10/	AC/DC	Palace Theater	Albany
1979	6/6/	Journey	Palace Theater	Albany
1979	5/10/	Cheap Trick	Palace Theater	Albany
1979	3/25/	Elvis Costello & The Attractions	Palace Theater	Albany
1979	2/22/	The Kinks	Palace Theater	Albany
1979	1/16/	Rush	Palace Theater	Albany
1979	1/16/	Starz	Palace Theater	Albany
1979	11/18/	Jefferson Starship	RPI Fieldhouse	Troy
1979	5/27/	Supertramp	RPI Fieldhouse	Troy
1979	11/8/	Jefferson Starship	RPI Fieldhouse	Troy
1980	5/7/	Gentle Giant	Hullabaloo	Rensselaer
1980	11/29/	Captain Beefheart & His Magic Band	JB Scott's Theater	Albany
1980	11/22/	Think Lizzy	JB Scott's Theater	Albany
1980	10/28/	Frank Zappa	Palace Theater	Albany
1980	7/27/	Jerry Garcia Band	Palace Theater	Albany

1980	4/28/	Bob Dylan	Palace Theater	Albany
1980	4/27/	Bob Dylan	Palace Theater	Albany
1980	3/9/	The Kinks	Palace Theater	Albany
1980	3/8/	Aerosmith	Alive at Five	Albany
1980	3/3/	UFO	Palace Theater	Albany
1980	2/13/	Jerry Garcia Band	Palace Theater	Albany
1980	2/3/	Blue Oyster Cult	Palace Theater	Albany
1980	1/23/	Max Webster	Palace Theater	Albany
1980	1/23/	Rush	Palace Theater	Albany
1980	1/22/	Max Webster	Palace Theater	Albany
1980	1/22/	Rush	Palace Theater	Albany
1980	9/18/	Billy Idol	Knickerbocker Arena	Albany
1980	Apr 2,	Frank Zappa	RPI Fieldhouse	Troy
1980	4/26/	Frank Zappa	RPI Fieldhouse	Troy
1981	12/12/	Todd Rundgren	JB Scott's Theater	Albany
1981	11/14/	David Crosby	JB Scott's Theater	Albany
1981	11/13/	U2	Jb Scott's Theater	Albany
1981	11/4/	Jerry Garcia Band	Palace Theater	Albany
1981	10/9/	Alice Cooper	Palace Theater	Albany
1981	10/2/	Blackfoot	Palace Theater	Albany
1981	10/2/	Def Leppard	Palace Theater	Albany
1981	7/21/	Iron Maiden	Palace Theater	Albany
1981	7/19/	Judas Priest	Palace Theater	Albany
1981	5/23/	U2	JB Scott's Theater	Albany
1981	5/12/	Rainbow	Palace Theater	Albany
1981	5/12/	Pat Travers	Palace Theater	Albany
1981	2/25/	Rainbow	JB Scott's Theater	Albany
1981	2/22/	Utopia	Jb Scott's Theater	Albany
1981	3/8/	Cheap Trick	RPI Fieldhouse	Troy
1981	3/8/	UFO	RPI Fieldhouse	Troy
1981	3/8/	Cheap Trick	RPI Fieldhouse	Troy

1982	3/2/	King Crimson	Hullabaloo	Rensselaer
1982	12/10/	Stray Cats	SUNYA	Albany
1982	11/23/	R.E.M.	The Chateau Lounge	Albany
1982	9/23/	Blue Oyster Cult	Palace Theater	Albany
1982	9/23/	Aldo Nova	Palace Theater	Albany
1982	8/17/	Roy Buchanan	JB Scott's Theater	Albany
1982	6/2/	Black Flag	Unknown	Albany
1982	5/1/	Squeeze	SUNYA	Albany
1982	4/25/	Uriah Heap	Unknown	Albany
1982	10/9/	David Johansen	RPI West Hall Auditorium	Troy
1982	10/3/	The Clash	RPI Fieldhouse	Troy
1982	10/3/	Clash	RPI Fieldhouse	Troy
1982	8/25/	J. Geils Band	SPAC	Saratoga
1982	8/25/	The Motels	SPAC	Saratoga
1983	12/11/	Billy Idol	SUNYA	Albany
1983	11/11/	Billy Idol	SUNYA	Albany
1983	10/23/	The Band	Palace Theater	Albany
1983	10/11/	Hot Tuna	Palace Theater	Albany
1983	10/4/	Bryan Adams	Unknown	Albany
1983	6/2/	Jerry Lee Lewis	Unknown	Albany
1983	5/7/	Robert Hazard	SUNYA	Albany
1983	5/7/	David Johansen	SUNYA	Albany
1983	5/7/	U2	SUNYA	Albany
1983	4/20/	Jorma Kaukonen	Page Hall	Albany
1983	4/10/	Bryan Adams	Unknown	Albany
1983	3/19/	Jerry Lee Lewis	Linda Norris Auditorium	Albany
1983	2/28/	Quiet Riot	Palace Theater	Albany
1984	11/14/	Slayer	Hudson River Cafe	Albany
1984	11/5/	Santana	Palace Theater	Albany

Year	Date	Artist	Venue	City
1984	7/20/	Twisted Sister	Palace Theater	Albany
1984	7/17/	Sammy Davis Jr	Colonie Coliseum	Latham
1984	7/7/	Ted Nugent	Palace Theater	Albany
1984	6/7/	Alcatraz	Palace Theater	Albany
1984	6/7/	Ted Nugent	Palace Theater	Albany
1984	3/21/	Pablo Cruise	Palace Theater	Albany
1984	3/1/	Black Sabbath	Palace Theater	Albany
1984	3/1/	Helix	Palace Theater	Albany
1984	2/24/	Blue Oyster Cult	Palace Theater	Albany
1984	2/24/	Girlschool	Palace Theater	Albany
1984	11/9/	Cyndi Lauper	RPI Fieldhouse	Troy
1985	12/12/	Roger Daltry	Palace Theater	Albany
1985	11/29/	The Hooters	JB Scott's Theater	Albany
1985	11/22/	Stevie Ray Vaughan	JB Scott's Theater	Albany
1985	11/6/	Al Di Meola	Palace Theater	Albany
1985	10/25/	Ray Charles	Palace Theater	Albany
1985	10/25/	Haven	JB Scott's Theater	Albany
1985	10/18/	Blue Oyster Cult	JB Scott's Theater	Albany
1985	10/18/	Kix	JB Scott's Theater	Albany
1985	9/13/	The Marshall Tucker Band	Jb Scott's Theater	Albany
1985	8/25/	R.E.M.	JB Scott's Theater	Albany
1985	8/12/	Stevie Ray Vaughan	Palace Theater	Albany
1985	6/15/	Trouble	New York Cafe	Albany
1985	5/4/	The Tubes	SUNYA	Albany
1985	5/4/	Utopia	SUNYA	Albany
1985	4/14/	Julian Lennon	Palace Theater	Albany
1985	3/21/	Pablo Cruise	Palace Theater	Albany
1985	3/21/	UB40	Palace Theater	Albany
1985	2/25/	Anthrax	Unknown	Albany
1985	10/9/	The Motels	RPI Fieldhouse	Troy
1985	10/9/	Supertramp	RPI Fieldhouse	Troy

Year	Date	Artist	Venue	City
1985	9/10/	Cheap Trick	RPI Fieldhouse	Troy
1985	9/10/	Heart	RPI Fieldhouse	Troy
1985	9/4/	Dio	RPI Fieldhouse	Troy
1985	8/15/	Neil Young	RPI Fieldhouse	Troy
1985	5/17/	The Beach Boys	RPI Fieldhouse	Troy
1985	5/17/	NRBQ	RPI Fieldhouse	Troy
1985	4/17/	George Thorogood & The Destroyers	RPI Fieldhouse	Troy
1985	5/17/	Beach Boys	RPI Fieldhouse	Troy
1985	9/4/	Ronnie James Dio	RPI Fieldhouse	Troy
1985	9/10/	Heart/Cheap Trick	RPI Fieldhouse	Troy
1985	10/9/	Supertramp	RPI Fieldhouse	Troy
1985	11/16/	Starship/Night Ranger	RPI Fieldhouse	Troy
1986	11/15/	Alice Cooper	Palace Theater	Albany
1986	11/15/	Vinnie Vincent Invasion	Palace Theater	Albany
1986	10/26/	Game Theory	Club 288	Albany
1986	7/26/	Blue Oyster Cult	JB Scott's Theater	Albany
1986	7/13/	Anthrax	Unknown	Albany
1986	6/20/	Ramones	JB Scott's Theater	Albany
1986	5/29/	UFO	JB Scott's Theater	Albany
1986	5/16/	Armored Saint	Unknown	Albany
1986	5/16/	Fates Warning	Unknown	Albany
1986	April	Black Flag	Unknown	Albany
1986	4/3/	Cheap Trick	JB Scott's Theater	Albany
1986	4/3/	Todd Rundgren	JB Scott's Theater	Albany
1986	1/24/	Pat Travers	JB Scott's Theater	Albany
1986	1/3/	Charlie Sexton	JB Scott's Theater	Albany
1986	11/30/	Stevie Ray Vaughan	RPI Fieldhouse	Troy
1986	11/2/	Crosby, Stills & Nash	RPI Fieldhouse	Troy
1986	9/24/	Neil Young	RPI Fieldhouse	Troy
1986	7/29/	Judas Priest	RPI Fieldhouse	Troy
1986	4/22/	Bobby McFerrin	RPI Fieldhouse	Troy

Year	Date	Artist	Venue	City
1986	4/22/	Robin Williams	RPI Fieldhouse	Troy
1986	4/11/	The Fools	RPI Fieldhouse	Troy
1986	4/11/	Southside Johnny & The Ashbury Jukes	RPI Fieldhouse	Troy
1986	2/24/	Pat Benatar	RPI Fieldhouse	Troy
1986	7/29/	Judas Priest	RPI Fieldhouse	Troy
1986	9/24/	Neil Young	RPI Fieldhouse	Troy
1986	10/10/	Monkees	RPI Fieldhouse	Troy
1986	11/30/	Stevie Ray Vaughan	RPI Fieldhouse	Troy
1987	12/2/	The Alarm	Palace Theater	Albany
1987	11/17/	John Entwistle	Palace Theater	Albany
1987	11/12/	Squeeze	Palace Theater	Albany
1987	10/29/	The Brandos	Unknown	Albany
1987	10/29/	INXS	Palace Theater	Albany
1987	10/1/	EZO	Unknown	Albany
1987	10/21/	Guns N Roses	Unknown	Albany
1987	10/12/	Marillion	Palace Theater	Albany
1987	8/30/	Gary Moore	Saratoga Winners	Cohoes
1987	7/21/	Saint Vitus	Unknown	Albany
1987	7/3/	Frehley's Comet	Palace Theater	Albany
1987	7/3/	White Lion	Palace Theater	Albany
1987	5/29/	Anthrax	Palace Theater	Albany
1987	5/29/	Metal Church	Palace Theater	Albany
1987	5/28/	Megadeth	Colonie Coliseum	Latham
1987	5/28/	Necros	Colonie Coliseum	Latham
1987	5/28/	Overkill	Colonie Coliseum	Latham
1987	4/30/	Sonic Youth	QE2	Albany
1987	3/7/	Eddie Money	Palace Theater	Albany
1987	Feb	Saxon	Saratoga Winners	Cohoes
1987	12/15/	Yes	RPI Fieldhouse	Troy
1987	11/13/	Alice Cooper	RPI Fieldhouse	Troy

Year	Date	Artist	Venue	City
1987	11/13/	Faster Pussycat	RPI Fieldhouse	Troy
1987	11/12/	McAuley-Schenker Group	RPI Fieldhouse	Troy
1987	11/12/	Rush	RPI Fieldhouse	Troy
1987	11/10/	Jethro Tull	RPI Fieldhouse	Troy
1987	8/14/	Motley Crue	RPI Fieldhouse	Troy
1987	8/14/	Whitesnake	RPI Fieldhouse	Troy
1987	4/27/	Bad Company	RPI Fieldhouse	Troy
1987	4/27/	Deep Purple	RPI Fieldhouse	Troy
1987	4/17/	Bestie Boys	RPI Fieldhouse	Troy
1987	4/17/	Public Enemy	RPI Fieldhouse	Troy
1987	4/10/	Bon Jovi	RPI Fieldhouse	Troy
1987	4/10/	Cinderella	RPI Fieldhouse	Troy
1987	1/29/	Raven	RPI Fieldhouse	Troy
1987	1/29/	Slayer	RPI Fieldhouse	Troy
1987	1/29/	W.A.S.P.	RPI Fieldhouse	Troy
1987	1/11/	Iron Maiden	RPI Fieldhouse	Troy
1987	1/11/	Yngwie J. Mamsteen	RPI Fieldhouse	Troy
1987	4/10/	Bon Jovi	RPI Fieldhouse	Troy
1987	8/14/	Motley Crue	RPI Fieldhouse	Troy
1987	10/10/	Hooters	RPI Fieldhouse	Troy
1987	11/10/	Jethro Tull	RPI Fieldhouse	Troy
1987	11/12/	Rush	RPI Fieldhouse	Troy
1987	11/13/	Alice Cooper	RPI Fieldhouse	Troy
1987	12/15/	Rush	RPI Fieldhouse	Troy
1988	11/10/	King Diamond	Saratoga Winners	Cohoes
1988	11/1/	Red Hot Chili Peppers	QE2	Albany
1988	7/12/	Yngwie J. Mamsteen	Palace Theater	Albany
1988	5/18/	Zondiac Mindwaro and the Love Reaction	Saratoga Winners	Cohoes
1988	5/18/	U,D.O.	Saratoga Winners	Cohoes
1988	4/26/	Megadeth	Unknown	Albany

Year	Date	Artist	Venue	City
1988	4/26/	Sanctuary	Unknown	Albany
1988	4/26/	Warlock	Unknown	Albany
1988	2/17/	Armored Saint	Saratoga Winners	Cohoes
1988	2/2/	Frank Zappa	Palace Theater	Albany
1988	1/26/	Game Theory	QE2	Albany
1988	11/5/	Jimmy Page	RPI Fieldhouse	Troy
1988	10/18/	Robert Plant	RPI Fieldhouse	Troy
1988	7/16/	Frehley's Comet	RPI Fieldhouse	Troy
1988	7/16/	Iron Maiden	RPI Fieldhouse	Troy
1988	6/23/	REO Speedwagon	RPI Fieldhouse	Troy
1988	2/6/	Sting	RPI Fieldhouse	Troy
1988	2/6/	Sting	RPI Fieldhouse	Troy
1989	12/20/	Bad English	Saratoga Winners	Cohoes
1989	12/20/	Saraya	Saratoga Winners	Cohoes
1989	11/15/	King Diamond	Saratoga Winners	Cohoes
1989	7/27/	Joe Jackson	Palace Theater	Albany
1989	5/11/	Phish	Pauly's Hotel	Albany
1989	4/15/	Spin Doctors	Reality Fest	Albany
1989	1/24/	Cheap Trick	Palace Theater	Albany
1989	1/24/	House of Lords	Palace Theater	Albany
1989	11/12/	Stevie Ray Vaughan	RPI Fieldhouse	Troy
1989	10/27/	Bob Dylan	RPI Fieldhouse	Troy
1989	10/24/	Great White	RPI Fieldhouse	Troy
1989	10/24/	Tesla	RPI Fieldhouse	Troy
1989	10/23/	Jethro Tull	RPI Fieldhouse	Troy
1989	5/9/	Rod Stewart	RPI Fieldhouse	Troy
1989	5/8/	Anthrax	RPI Fieldhouse	Troy
1989	5/8/	Exodus	RPI Fieldhouse	Troy
1989	5/8/	Helloween	RPI Fieldhouse	Troy

Year	Date	Artist	Venue	City
1989	5/4/	Cinderella	RPI Fieldhouse	Troy
1989	5/4/	Winger	RPI Fieldhouse	Troy
1989	4/9/	Kix	RPI Fieldhouse	Troy
1989	4/9/	Ratt	RPI Fieldhouse	Troy
1989	3/15/	Metallica	RPI Fieldhouse	Troy
1989	3/15/	Queensryche	RPI Fieldhouse	Troy
1989	3/15/	Metallica	RPI Fieldhouse	Troy
1989	5/9/	Rod Stewart	RPI Fieldhouse	Troy
1989	10/23/	Jethro Tull	RPI Fieldhouse	Troy
1989	10/27/	Bob Dylan	RPI Fieldhouse	Troy
1990	12/18/	Billy Joel	Knickerbocker Arena	Albany
1990	12/9/	Billy Joel	Knickerbocker Arena	Albany
1990	11/29/	The Black Crowes	Saratoga Winners	Cohoes
1990	11/17/	Fleetwood Mac	Knickerbocker Arena	Albany
1990	11/16/	Pantera	Unknown	Albany
1990	11/16/	Poison	Knickerbocker Arena	Albany
1990	11/16/	Prong	Unknown	Albany
1990	11/16/	Warrant	Knickerbocker Arena	Albany
1990	11/6/	Iggy Pop	Saratoga Winners	Cohoes
1990	10/28/	Danzig	Saratoga Winners	Cohoes
1990	10/28/	Trouble	Saratoga Winners	Cohoes
1990	10/27/	Bad Company	Knickerbocker Arena	Albany
1990	10/27/	Dam Yankees	Knickerbocker Arena	Albany
1990	9/25/	Midnight Oil	Palace Theater	Albany
1990	9/19/	The Allman Brothers Band	Knickerbocker Arena	Albany
1990	9/18/	Faith No More	Knickerbocker Arena	Albany
1990	9/10/	Pantera	Unknown	Albany
1990	9/7/	Exodus	Saratoga Winners	Cohoes
1990	9/7/	Pantera	Saratoga Winners	Cohoes

1990	9/7/	Suicidal Tendencies	Saratoga Winners	Cohoes
1990	8/25/	Janet Jackson	Knickerbocker Arena	Albany
1990	7/7/	KISS	Knickerbocker Arena	Albany
1990	7/7/	Little Caesar	Knickerbocker Arena	Albany
1990	7/7/	Slaughter	Knickerbocker Arena	Albany
1990	7/5/	Alannah Myles	Knickerbocker Arena	Albany
1990	7/5/	Robert Plant	Knickerbocker Arena	Albany
1990	6/14/	Marillion	Saratoga Winners	Cohoes
1990	6/2/	Mr. Big	Knickerbocker Arena	Albany
1990	6/2/	Rush	Knickerbocker Arena	Albany
1990	5/23/	Savatage	Saratoga Winners	Cohoes
1990	5/4/	The Kinks	Palace Theater	Albany
1990	4/11/	Faster Pussycat	Knickerbocker Arena	Albany
1990	4/11/	Motley Crue	Knickerbocker Arena	Albany
1990	3/26/	Grateful Dead	Knickerbocker Arena	Albany
1990	3/25/	Grateful Dead	Knickerbocker Arena	Albany
1990	3/24/	Grateful Dead	Knickerbocker Arena	Albany
1990	2/15/	Whitesnake	Knickerbocker Arena	Albany
1990	1/30/	Frank Sinatra	Knickerbocker Arena	Albany
1990	9/29/	They Might Be Giants	RPI Fieldhouse	Troy
1990	9/29/	They Might Be Giants	McNeil Room, RPI	Troy
1991	12/12/	Vinnie Moore	Knickerbocker Arena	Albany
1991	12/12/	Rush	Knickerbocker Arena	Albany
1991	12/1/	Spin Doctors	Bogies	Albany
1991	11/20/	Paula Abdul	Knickerbocker Arena	Albany
1991	11/20/	Color Me Badd	Knickerbocker Arena	Albany
1991	11/16/	Jerry Garcia Band	Knickerbocker Arena	Albany
1991	11/15/	Jethro Tull	Knickerbocker Arena	Albany
1991	11/13/	Frank Sinatra	Knickerbocker Arena	Albany

1991	10/24/	Nuclear Assault	Saratoga Winners	Cohoes
1991	10/23/	Alice in Chains	Knickerbocker Arena	Albany
1991	10/23/	Van Halen	Knickerbocker Arena	Albany
1991	10/11/	James Cotton Blues Band	Bogies	Albany
1991	9/23/	Van Halen	Knickerbocker Arena	Albany
1991	8/21/	The Beach Boys	Knickerbocker Arena	Albany
1991	7/28/	Queensryche	Knickerbocker Arena	Albany
1991	7/28/	Suicidal Tendencies	Knickerbocker Arena	Albany
1991	7/5/	AC/DC	Knickerbocker Arena	Albany
1991	7/5/	L.A. Guns	Knickerbocker Arena	Albany
1991	5/8/	Bob Dylan	Palace Theater	Albany
1991	4/25/	Yes	Knickerbocker Arena	Albany
1991	4/22/	Great White	Knickerbocker Arena	Albany
1991	4/22/	Scorpions	Knickerbocker Arena	Albany
1991	4/22/	Trixter	Knickerbocker Arena	Albany
1991	3/25/	Grateful Dead	Knickerbocker Arena	Albany
1991	3/23/	Grateful Dead	Knickerbocker Arena	Albany
1991	3/10/	Fugazi	Saratoga Winners	Cohoes
1991	2/5/	The Black Crowes	Knickerbocker Arena	Albany
1991	2/5/	ZZ Top	Knickerbocker Arena	Albany
1991	1/	Anthrax	Knickerbocker Arena	Albany
1991	1/22/	Iron Maiden	Knickerbocker Arena	Albany
1991	1/14/	Judas Priest	Knickerbocker Arena	Albany
1991	1/14/	Megadeth	Knickerbocker Arena	Albany
1991	11/5/	Pearl Jam	RPI Fieldhouse	Troy
1991	11/5/	Red Hot Chili Peppers	RPI Fieldhouse	Troy
1991	11/5/	The Smashing Pumpkins	RPI Fieldhouse	Troy
1991	9/27/	Anthrax	RPI Fieldhouse	Troy
1991	9/27/	Primus	RPI Fieldhouse	Troy
1991	9/27/	Public Enemy	RPI Fieldhouse	Troy

Year	Date	Artist	Venue	City
1991	4/27/	Jane's Addiction	RPI Fieldhouse	Troy
1991	2/11/	Slayer	RPI Fieldhouse	Troy
1991	2/11/	Testament	RPI Fieldhouse	Troy
1991	2/9/	Social Distortion	RPI Fieldhouse	Troy
1991	2/9/	Sonic Youth	RPI Fieldhouse	Troy
1991	2/9/	Neil Young	RPI Fieldhouse	Troy
1991	2/9/	Neil Young & Crazy Horse	RPI Fieldhouse	Troy
1991	2/9/	Sonic Youth	RPI Fieldhouse	Troy
1991	11/5/	Red Hot Chili Peppers	RPI Fieldhouse	Troy
1991	11/5/	Smashing Pumpkins	RPI Fieldhouse	Troy
1991	11/5/	Pearl Jam	RPI Fieldhouse	Troy
1992	12/5/	Bryan Adams	Knickerbocker Arena	Albany
1992	12/5/	Mr. Big	Knickerbocker Arena	Albany
1992	11/20/	Phish	Palace Theater	Albany
1992	11/15/	Ween	Bogies	Albany
1992	11/8/	Tori Amos	Page Hall	Albany
1992	10/29/	Spin Doctors	Palace Theater	Albany
1992	10/28/	Def Leppard	Knickerbocker Arena	Albany
1992	10/16/	Black Sabbath	Palace Theater	Albany
1992	10/16/	Exodus	Palace Theater	Albany
1992	10/16/	Skew Siskin	Palace Theater	Albany
1992	10/7/	Jethro Tull	Palace Theater	Albany
1992	10/4/	Faith No More	Palace Theater	Albany
1992	10/4/	Helmet	Palace Theater	Albany
1992	10/1/	Dream Theater	Saratoga Winners	Cohoes
1992	9/25/	Elton John	Knickerbocker Arena	Albany
1992	9/2/	Neil Diamond	Knickerbocker Arena	Albany
1992	9/1/	Neil Diamond	Knickerbocker Arena	Albany
1992	8/22/	The Black Crowes	Palace Theater	Albany
1992	8/2/	Emerson, Lake & Palmer	Palace Theater	Albany

1992	7/14/	Spin Doctors	Saratoga Winners	Cohoes
1992	6/12/	Grateful Dead	Knickerbocker Arena	Albany
1992	6/11/	Grateful Dead	Knickerbocker Arena	Albany
1992	5/30/	Spin Doctors	Saratoga Winners	Cohoes
1992	4/15/	They Might Be Giants	Unknown	Albany
1992	Ap 12	The Moody Blues	Palace Theater	Albany
1992	3/22/	The Mighty Mighty Bosstones	Bogies	Albany
1992	3/21/	Pixies	Knickerbocker Arena	Albany
1992	3/21/	U2	Knickerbocker Arena	Albany
1992	2/29/	Spin Doctors	Bogies	Albany
1992	2/28/	Metallica	Knickerbocker Arena	Albany
1992	4/27/	Steve Miller Band	RPI Fieldhouse	Troy
1993	11/20/	Best Kissers in the World	Saratoga Winners	Cohoes
1993	11/12/	Rod Stewart	Knickerbocker Arena	Albany
1993	11/11/	I Mother Earth	Saratoga Winners	Cohoes
1993	11/11/	My Sister's Machine	Saratoga Winners	Cohoes
1993	11/8/	Neil Diamond	Knickerbocker Arena	Albany
1993	11/3/	Jerry Garcia Band	Knickerbocker Arena	Albany
1993	10/1/	Black 47	Recreation and Convocation Center	Albany
1993	10/1/	Cracker	Recreation and Convocation Center	Albany
1993	10/1/	The Mighty Mighty Bosstones	Recreation and Convocation Center	Albany
1993	10/1/	Pere Ubu	Recreation and Convocation Center	Albany
1993	10/1/	They Might Be Giants	Recreation and Convocation Center	Albany
1993	9/23/	Steely Dan	Knickerbocker Arena	Albany
1993	9/20/	Fugazi	Recreation and Convocation Center	Albany
1993	9/18/	4 Non Blondes	Knickerbocker Arena	Albany
1993	9/1/	Aerosmith	Knickerbocker Arena	Albany

1993	9/19/	Cathedral	Saratoga Winners	Cohoes
1993	9/8/	Flotsam and Jetsam	Saratoga Winners	Cohoes
1993	9/8/	Mercyful Fate	Saratoga Winners	Cohoes
1993	8/19/	Billy Ray Cyrus	Knickerbocker Arena	Albany
1993	7/25/	Winger	Saratoga Winners	Cohoes
1993	5/16/	Dream Theater	Palace Theater	Albany
1993	5/6/	Phish	Palace Theater	Albany
1993	5/5/	Phish	Palace Theater	Albany
1993	4/26/	Digable Planets	Recreation and Convocation Center	Albany
1993	4/20/	Flotsam and Jetsam	Saratoga Winners	Albany
1993	3/29/	Grateful Dead	Knickerbocker Arena	Albany
1993	3/28/	Grateful Dead	Knickerbocker Arena	Albany
1993	3/27/	Grateful Dead	Knickerbocker Arena	Albany
1993	3/19/	Blind Melon	Saratoga Winners	Cohoes
1993	3/12/	Pantera	Palace Theater	Albany
1993	3/12/	Sacred Reich	Palace Theater	Albany
1993	2/16/	Bon Jovi	Knickerbocker Arena	Albany
1993	1/22/	Megadeth	Knickerbocker Arena	Albany
1993	1/22/	Stone Temple Pilots	Knickerbocker Arena	Albany
1994	12/18/	Aerosmith	Knickerbocker Arena	Albany
1994	12/18/	Jackyl	Knickerbocker Arena	Albany
1994	12/4/	The Jim Rose Circus Sideshow	Knickerbocker Arena	Albany
1994	12/4/	Marilyn Manson	Knickerbocker Arena	Albany
1994	12/4/	Nine Inch Nails	Knickerbocker Arena	Albany
1994	11/11/	Candlebox	Recreation and Convocation Center	Albany
1994	11/11/	The Flaming Lips	Recreation and Convocation Center	Albany
1994	11/11/	Sweet Water	Recreation and Convocation Center	Albany
1994	11/4/	Fates Warning	Saratoga Winners	Albany

1994	11/3/	The Cranberries	Recreation and Convocation Center	Albany
1994	11/3/	Gigolo Aunts	Recreation and Convocation Center	Albany
1994	11/3/	MC 900 Ft Jesus	Recreation and Convocation Center	Albany
1994	10/23/	Moe	Kicks Nightclub	Albany
1994	10/14/	Bob Dylan	Palace Theater	Albany
1994	10/3/	Live	Saratoga Winners	Cohoes
1994	10/2/	Dan Fogelberg	Palace Theater	Albany
1994	7/1/	The Moody Blues	Knickerbocker Arena	Albany
1994	6/28/	Travis Tritt	Knickerbocker Arena	Albany
1994	6/27/	Tori Amos	Palace Theater	Albany
1994	6/23/	Billy Ray Cyrus	Riverfront	Albany
1994	6/16/	Biohazard	Knickerbocker Arena	Albany
1994	6/16/	Pantera	Knickerbocker Arena	Albany
1994	6/16/	Sepultura	Knickerbocker Arena	Albany
1994	5/3/	Candlebox	Knickerbocker Arena	Albany
1994	5/3/	Rush	Knickerbocker Arena	Albany
1994	4/18/	Red Red Meat	Recreation and Convocation Center	Albany
1994	4/18/	The Smashing Pumpkins	Recreation and Convocation Center	Albany
1994	3/13/	De La Soul	Recreation and Convocation Center	Albany
1994	3/13/	A Tribe Called Quest	Recreation and Convocation Center	Albany
1994	3/11/	I Mother Earth	Saratoga Winners	Cohoes
1994	3/11/	Mutha's Day Out	Saratoga Winners	Cohoes
1994	3/9/	Clutch	Saratoga Winners	Cohoes
1994	3/9/	Fear Factory	Saratoga Winners	Cohoes
1994	3/9/	Fudge Tunnel	Saratoga Winners	Cohoes
1994	3/9/	Sepultura	Saratoga Winners	Cohoes

1994	3/2/	Widespread Panic	Saratoga Winners	Cohoes
1994	1/24/	Janet Jackson	Knickerbocker Arena	Albany
1994	1/20/	Billy Joel	Knickerbocker Arena	Albany
1994	1/18/	Billy Joel	Knickerbocker Arena	Albany
1995	12/9/	Phish	Knickerbocker Arena	Albany
1995	12/9/	Moe	Valentines Music Hall	Albany
1995	11/30/	White Zombie	Unknown	Albany
1995	11/18/	Primus	Recreation and Convocation Center	Albany
1995	11/17/	Candlebox	Recreation and Convocation Center	Albany
1995	11/17/	Our Lady Peace	Recreation and Convocation Center	Albany
1995	11/17/	Sponge	Recreation and Convocation Center	Albany
1995	10/28/	Marilyn Manson	Saratoga Winners	Cohoes
1995	10/8/	Mike Watt and he Crew of the Flying Saucer	Bogies	Albany
1995	10/	Blues Traveler	Recreation and Convocation Center	Albany
1995	9/22/	Moe	Valentines Music Hall	Albany
1995	9/1/	Dionne Farris	Recreation and Convocation Center	Albany
1995	9/1/	Dave Matthews Band	Recreation and Convocation Center	Albany
1995	7/26/	Radiohead	Saratoga Winners	Cohoes
1995	7/21/	Queensryche	Knickerbocker Arena	Albany
1995	7/21/	Type O Negative	Knickerbocker Arena	Albany
1995	7/13/	Moe	Alive at Five	Albany
1995	7/13/	Moe	Valentines Music Hall	Albany
1995	6/22/	Grateful Dead	Knickerbocker Arena	Albany
1995	6/22/	Korn	Saratoga Winners	Albany
1995	6/22/	Sugar Ray	Saratoga Winners	Albany
1995	6/21/	Grateful Dead	Knickerbocker Arena	Albany
1995	6/20/	Goo Goo Dolls	Unknown	Albany

1995	6/20/	Luscious Jackson	Knickerbocker Arena	Albany
1995	6/20/	R.E.M.	Knickerbocker Arena	Albany
1995	5/14/	Belly	Washington Park	Albany
1995	5/7/	Van Halen	Knickerbocker Arena	Albany
1995	5/6/	Moe	Bogies	Albany
1995	3/25/	Sheryl Crow	Recreation and Convocation Center	Albany
1995	3/25/	Freddy Johnson	Recreation and Convocation Center	Albany
1995	3/23/	Joe Cocker	Palace Theater	Albany
1995	3/23/	Keb' Mo'	Palace Theater	Albany
1995	3/9/	Live	Recreation and Convocation Center	Albany
1995	3/9/	Love Spit Love	Recreation and Convocation Center	Albany
1995	3/9/	Sponge	Recreation and Convocation Center	Albany
1995	3/6/	Marilyn Manson	QE2	Albany
1995	2/9/	They Might Be Giants	Saratoga Winners	Cohoes
1995	2/8/	Dave Matthews Band	Palace Theater	Albany
1995	12/2/	Moe	Phi Kappa Alpha	Troy
1996	11/29/	Deftones	Saratoga Winners	Cohoes
1996	11/22/	The Electric Hellfire Club	Saratoga Winners	Cohoes
1996	11/22/	Fear Factory	Saratoga Winners	Cohoes
1996	11/18/	The Who	Knickerbocker Arena	Albany
1996	11/9/	Type O Negative	Saratoga Winners	Cohoes
1996	11/2/	The Smashing Pumpkins	Knickerbocker Arena	Albany
1996	10/26/	Mercyful Fate	Saratoga Winners	Cohoes
1996	10/26/	Overdose	Saratoga Winners	Cohoes
1996	10/25/	Moe	Saratoga Winners	Cohoes
1996	10/	Rush	Knickerbocker Arena	Albany

1996	10/18/	Rush	Knickerbocker Arena	Albany
1996	10/15/	The Black Crowes	Palace Theater	Albany
1996	10/12/	Deltones	Knickerbocker Arena	Albany
1996	10/12/	Kiss	Knickerbocker Arena	Albany
1996	10/10/	Boxing Gandhis	Knickerbocker Arena	Albany
1996	10/10/	Dave Matthews Band	Knickerbocker Arena	Albany
1996	9/27/	They Might Be Giants	Recreation and Convocation Center	Albany
1996	9/26/	Moe	Palace Theater	Albany
1996	9/11/	The Cure	Knickerbocker Arena	Albany
1996	9/26/	Moe	Palace Theater	Albany
1996	9/11/	The Cure	Knickerbocker Arena	Albany
1996	9/7/	AC/DC	Knickerbocker Arena	Albany
1996	8/28/	Deftones	Knickerbocker Arena	Albany
1996	8/28/	Pantera	Knickerbocker Arena	Albany
1996	8/28/	White Zombie	Knickerbocker Arena	Albany
1996	7/29/	AC/DC	Knickerbocker Arena	Albany
1996	6/30/	Anal Cunt	Bogies	Albany
1996	6/30/	Morpheus Descends	Bogies	Albany
1996	5/10/	Tori Amos	Palace Theater	Albany
1996	4/28/	Ramones	Lincoln Park	Albany
1996	3/30/	Billy Joel	Palace Theater	Albany
1996	3/16/	Kreator	Saratoga Winners	Albany
1996	2/23/	Moe	Valentines Music Hall	Albany
1996	2/22/	Rod Stewart	Knickerbocker Arena	Albany
1996	2/11/	Red Hot Chili Peppers	Knickerbocker Arena	Albany
1996	1/22/	Ben Folds Five	Bogies	Albany
1996	1/10/	Marilyn Manson	Saratoga Winners	Cohoes
1996	2/13/	Loud Lucy	RPI Fieldhouse	Troy
1996	2/13/	Alanis Morissette	RPI Fieldhouse	Troy
1996	1/27/	Korn	RPI Fieldhouse	Troy

Year	Date	Artist	Venue	City
1996	1/27/	Ozzy Osbourne	RPI Fieldhouse	Troy
1996	1/27/	Ozzy Osbourne/Korn	RPI Fieldhouse	Troy
1996	2/11/	Red Hot Chili Peppers	RPI Fieldhouse	Troy
1996	2/13/	Alanis Morissette	RPI	Troy
1997	12/13/	Phish	Pepsi Arena	Albany
1997	12/12/	Phish	Pepsi Arena	Albany
1997	11/26/	Fleetwood Mac	Pepsi Arena	Albany
1997	10/31/	The Beach Boys	Pepsi Arena	Albany
1997	10/31/	From Good Homes	Palace Theater	Albany
1997	10/31/	Ratdog	Palace Theater	Albany
1997	10/26/	Grand Funk Railroad	Palace Theater	Albany
1997	10/21/	Yes	Palace Theater	Albany
1997	10/20/	Machine Head	QE2	Albany
1997	8/24/	Noisex	QE2	Albany
1997	8/15/	Exodus	Bogies	Albany
1997	7/25/	Machine Head	Saratoga Winners	Cohoes
1997	7/10/	No Doubt	Pepsi Arena	Albany
1997	6/28/	Misfits	Bogies	Albany
1997	6/14/	Wilco	Saratoga Winners	Albany
1997	4/30/	Barry Manilow	Pepsi Arena	Albany
1997	4/18/	Bob Dylan	Recreation and Convocation Center	Albany
1997	4/16/	Moe	Saratoga Winners	Cohoes
1997	4/12/	Garth Brooks	Pepsi Arena	Albany
1997	4/11/	Garth Brooks	Pepsi Arena	Albany
1997	4/10/	Garth Brooks	Pepsi Arena	Albany
1997	4/6/	Corrosion of Conformity	Pepsi Arena	Albany
1997	4/6/	Metallica	Pepsi Arena	Albany
1997	3/25/	Phil Collins	Pepsi Arena	Albany
1997	3/4/	Soul Coughing	Saratoga Winners	Cohoes

1997	7/13/	Queens of the Stone Age	Palace Theater	Albany
1997	7/11/	Snoop Dog	Upstate Concert Hall	Clifton Park
1997	7/10/	Lord Huron	Alive at Five	Albany
1997	7/7/	Attila	Upstate Concert Hall	Clifton Park
1997	7/7/	Born of Osiris	Upstate Concert Hall	Clifton Park
1997	7/7/	Get Scared	Upstate Concert Hall	Clifton Park
1997	7/6/	Syd Arthur	Hart Theater, The Egg	Albany
1997	7/6/	Trapt	Upstate Concert Hall	Clifton Park
1997	10/3/	Herbie Hancock & Wayne Shorter	Troy Savings Bank Music Hall	Troy
1997	2/18/	L7	RPI Fieldhouse	Troy
1997	2/18/	Marilyn Manson	RPI Fieldhouse	Troy
1997	2/17/	Live	RPI Fieldhouse	Troy
1997	2/18/	Live	RPI Fieldhouse	Troy
1997	2/18/	Marilyn Manson	RPI Fieldhouse	Troy
1998	12/29/	Aerosmith	Pepsi Arena	Albany
1998	12/29/	Candlebox	Palace Theater	Albany
1998	12/5/	Bela Fleck and the Flecktones	Pepsi Arena	Albany
1998	12/5/	Dave Matthews Band	Pepsi Arena	Albany
1998	12/1/	Celine Dion	Pepsi Arena	Albany
1998	11/25/	Phish	Pepsi Arena	Albany
1998	11/24/	Todd Rundgren	Northern Lights	Clifton Park
1998	11/15/	Econoline Crush	Pepsi Arena	Albany
1998	11/15/	Kiss	Pepsi Arena	Albany
1998	9/20/	You Am I	Valentines Music Hall	Albany
1998	9/15/	Elton John	Pepsi Arena	Albany
1998	9/11/	Hanson	Pepsi Arena	Albany
1998	8/23/	Cinderella	Valentines Music Hall	Albany
1998	8/21/	Floater	The Venetian Theater	Albany

1998	8/5/	Tori Amos	Palace Theater	Albany
1998	7/11/	Jimmy Page & Robert Plant	Pepsi Arena	Albany
1998	6/24/	Skinless	Valentines Music Hall	Albany
1998	6/9/	Fury of Five	Valentines	Albany
1998	6/8/	Vision of Disorder	Valentines	Albany
1998	6/3/	Schrodinger's Cat	Bogies	Albany
1998	5/8/	Foo Fighters	Page Hall	Albany
1998	5/8/	Projekct Two	Valentines Music Hall	Albany
1998	5/8/	Rocket From the Crypt	Page Hall	Albany
1998	5/7/	Jars Of Clay	Palace Theater	Albany
1998	4/26/	Moe	Recreation and Convocation Center	Albany
1998	4/18/	The Electric Hellfire Club	QE2	Albany
1998	4/10/	Ani DiFranco	Palace Theater	Albany
1998	3/28/	16 Horsepower	Recreation and Convocation Center	Albany
1998	3/28/	Ratdog	Recreation and Convocation Center	Albany
1998	1/13/	Aerosmith	Pepsi Arena	Albany
1998	1/13/	Kenny Wayne Shepherd	Pepsi Arena	Albany
1998	3/28/	There Might Be Giants	RPI Fieldhouse	Troy
1998	2/14/	Chuck Mangione	Troy Savings Bank Music Hall	Troy
1998	3/28/	They Might Be Giants	McNeil Room, RPI	Troy
1999	12/1/	Guster	Northern Lights	Clifton Park
1999	11/21/	Bruce Sprinsteen	Pepsi Arena	Albany
1999	11/20/	Bruce Sprinsteen	Pepsi Arena	Albany
1999	11/20/	Widespread Panic	Palace Theater	Albany
1999	11/13/	Beth Hart	Recreation and Convocation Center	Albany
1999	11/13/	Ratdog	Recreation and Convocation Center	Albany
1999	11/12/	Type O Negative	Unknown	Albany
1999	10/25/	Primus	Pepsi Arena	Albany

1999	10/10/	Phish	Pepsi Arena	Albany
1999	10/9/	Phish	Pepsi Arena	Albany
1999	8/31/	Little Feat	Empire State Plaza	Albany
1999	8/28/	Jethro Tull	Palace Theater	Albany
1999	8/10/	Roger Waters	Pepsi Arena	Albany
1999	7/20/	Bob Dylan	Pepsi Arena	Albany
1999	7/20/	Paul Simon	Pepsi Arena	Albany
1999	7/16/	Cher	Pepsi Arena	Albany
1999	6/30/	Night Ranger	Pepsi Arena	Albany
1999	6/30/	Ted Nugent	Pepsi Arena	Albany
1999	6/30/	Quiet Riot	Pepsi Arena	Albany
1999	6/30/	Slaughter	Pepsi Arena	Albany
1999	6/29/	Nevermore	Northern Lights	Clifton Park
1999	6/26/	Nevermore	Unknown	Albany
1999	6/5/	Buckcherry	Altamont Fairgrounds	Altamont
1999	6/5/	The Flys	Altamont Fairgrounds	Altamont
1999	6/5/	Fuel	Altamont Fairgrounds	Altamont
1999	6/5/	Local H	Altamont Fairgrounds	Altamont
1999	6/5/	Sponge	Altamont Fairgrounds	Altamont
1999	6/5/	Rob Zombie	Altamont Fairgrounds	Altamont
1999	5/15/	Trey Anastasio Band	Palace Theater	Albany
1999	4/22/	Cheap Trick	Palace Theater	Albany
1999	3/25/	Better Than Ezra	Northern Lights	Clifton Park
1999	3/25/	Train	Northern Lights	Clifton Park
1999	3/23/	Gov't Mule	Northern Lights	Cohoes
1999	3/15/	NSYNC	Pepsi Arena	Albany
1999	3/13/	Billy Joel	Pepsi Arena	Albany

1999	3/8/	The Black Crowes	Palace Theater	Albany
1999	2/25/	Rod Stewart	Pepsi Arena	Albany
1999	3/2/	The Living End	RPI Fieldhouse	Troy
1999	3/2/	The Offspring	RPI Fieldhouse	Troy
1999	3/2/	Ozomatli	RPI Fieldhouse	Troy
1999	2/22/	Bob Dylan	RPI Fieldhouse	Troy
1999	2/22/	Bob Dylan	RPI Fieldhouse	Troy
1999	3/22/	The Offspring	RPI Fieldhouse	Troy

This list is copyrighted 2020 by Don Rittner

If you are interested in the local music scene you can check out these excellent Facebook pages:

"N.Y. Capital District's Bands of the 60s, 70s, and 80s"
here: https://www.facebook.com/groups/1752542151638706

"80's/90's Albany Underground Punk, Hardcore & Alternative Music Scene"
here: https://www.facebook.com/groups/541070529266011

"THE "518 MUSIC SCENE"
here: https://www.facebook.com/groups/169296379888433

"Capital Area Music And Beyond Scene Thru The Decades"
here: https://www.facebook.com/groups/471307560144030